A MACBETH

In this adaptation of Shakespeare's great tragedy, Charles Marowitz succeeds in recapturing the excitement it must have had for its first audiences. Starting from the premise that Macbeth is a jinxed play that has rarely, if ever, received a successful 'straight' production, Marowitz restructures the play so that we are faced afresh with its core and its layers of meaning. His analysis of the play as being permeated with voodoo and witchcraft is a brilliant one and succeeds in transforming the play from something of largely academic interest into something vital and relevant with great dramatic impact for today's audiences. He has successfully produced this version in Wiesbaden, Rome, Paris and the Open Space Theatre, London, of which he is artistic director.

Of even more interest to many will be the exercises outlined in the introduction, which form a blueprint for 'collage' theatre, and Marowitz' penetrating and illuminating comments both about Macbeth and his rehearsal method for the play. The exercises for actors that he describes are likely to become regarded as standard for 'collage' theatre, in the same way as Stanislavsky's are for naturalistic theatre.

Charles Marowitz was born in New York. He spent a year at LAMDA and in the late fifties and early sixties ran an acting studio called In-Stage at the British Drama League. He started to formulate his ideas and theories about acting technique and 'collage' theatre at this time, which were developed by his collaboration with Peter Brook on the RSC Theatre of Cruelty season in 1964. The following year, he directed his collage version of Hamlet at the LAMDA Theatre, which was critically acclaimed and successfully shown all over Europe. This was later published. He founded the Open Space Theatre in London, of which he is artistic director, in 1968, and among the many new plays he has produced there are works by Paul Ableman, John Herbert and John Guare. Among his books are The Method As Means, a survey of acting technique, and The Theatre at Work, a symposium on modern theatre practice which he jointly edited with Simon Trussler.

PLAYSCRIPT 45
'a macbeth'
FREELY ADAPTED FROM SHAKESPEARE'S TRAGEDY

charles marowitz

CALDER AND BOYARS · LONDON

First published in Great Britain 1971 by
Calder and Boyars Limited
18 Brewer Street, London W1R 4AS

© Charles Marowitz 1971

The photographs in this volume are by John Haynes
and may not be reproduced without permission.

© John Haynes 1971

All performing rights in this adaptation are strictly
reserved and applications for performances should be
made to
Charles Marowitz, Open Space Theatre,
32 Tottenham Court Rd., London W.1.

No performance of the adaptation may be given unless
a licence has been obtained prior to rehearsal.

ALL RIGHTS RESERVED

ISBN 0 7145 0719 9 Cloth Edition
ISBN 0 7145 0720 2 Paper Edition

Any paperback edition of this book whether published
simultaneously with, or subsequent to, the hard bound
edition is sold subject to the condition that it shall not,
by way of trade, be lent, resold, hired out, or otherwise
disposed of, without the publishers' consent, in any form
of binding or cover other than that in which it is published.

Printed by photo-lithography
and made in Great Britain at
The Pitman Press, Bath.

For Thelma Holt who made me do it in Criccieth...

CONTENTS

INTRODUCTION 7

EXERCISES 16

A MACBETH 33

INTRODUCTION

Macbeth, as we all know, is a jinxed play. But what is a jinxed play? Is it simply a play that actors and directors have not managed to make work? Then surely Lear which critics have pronounced 'unactable' and 'impossible' is more jinxed than Macbeth. Or Hamlet which despite the frequency of revivals, very rarely manages to succeed.

But perhaps this is not what we mean when we say Macbeth is jinxed. Perhaps we simply mean the incidence of injury and catastrophe in regard to the play is remarkably high; that old troupers, their eyes still glazed with fright, can recount horrible events which occurred because the play's last line was actually spoken in rehearsal whereas anyone with sense knows it must not be uttered until the first night; that almost everyone connected with a production of Macbeth can recall some fall, some spasm, some unaccountable malady affecting one or another member of the cast; some unfortunate mummer who, out of disrespect or ignorance of the Macbeth curse, violated one of the many taboos attached to the play. (In Germany, whistling in the theatre is forbidden by written regulation. In England, whistling during a production of Macbeth is tantamount to to invoking the gods to hurl lightning on your head).

Shakespeare wrote approximately thirty-seven plays. Some are bright; some are dark; some are multi-coloured; some are clearly potboilers, others are considered masterpieces. But only one is jinxed.

Before the rehearsals of Macbeth began in London, I lost the actor earmarked for the lead role. At the very last moment I was obliged to cast someone else. I chose a very talented young actor I had met while teaching at a London drama-school. He was originally going to play Banquo. I explained the change-of-plan, asked him if he were game to tackle the part, and he agreed. Rehearsals began without incident.

After about the third day, the actor in question came to rehearsal in a clearly disturbed state. He had been to a party the night before; had smoked too much; stayed too long; got too tired. He found it difficult to concentrate. He began to shiver uncontrollably. The rehearsal was cancelled.

The following day he believed himself to be much better. The rehearsals began. When we reached the scene where Macbeth invites Banquo to the banquet, he became unaccountably frightened by the actor playing Banquo. He found it impossible to look into his face. We tried rehearsing with Banquo averting his gaze. The tension remained. He said afterward that the actor seemed to be glowering at him diabolically; taunting him with a cruel, obscene smile. The rehearsal was stopped.

Later in the day, when we began to rehearse the play's coda in which the entire company surrounds Macbeth and gradually swamps him, the actor became visibly distraught and slightly hysterical. At a point where the scene reaches an emotional climax, he fell over in a faint. Prior to that moment, he had been giving one of the most extraordinary and fascinating performances I have ever witnessed; acting in a manner which, if I were asked to describe in one word, I would call 'possessed'.

The following day the actor was brought to a doctor whose opinion was that because of personal stresses and the added pressure of a highly claustrophobic production, the actor was undergoing a slow nervous breakdown. We were advised to discontinue rehearsals. I said this was impossible, and we agreed to persevere a little longer. I confess to a certain callousness in my attitude. The actor was clearly unwell, but I was bewitched by what I had seen the day before and desperately wanted to see if this daemonic quality would recur.

As a result of daily care and attention, carefully organized breaks and constant surveillance, the actor managed to overcome whatever stress it was that was affecting him. We opened the play in Wiesbaden and later played it in London, Paris and Rome.

Discussing the breakdown afterward, neither he nor I could account for exact causes - although there was a great deal about which to speculate: girl-problems, financial worries, moving flat, tackling a major role immediately after drama-school, etc. We analysed all the possible causes. Fancifully, I suggested it might just have been a jinx; the well-known and much-dreaded <u>Macbeth</u> jinx. He laughed at this; so did I.

Lear is insurmountable, Macbeth incontrovertible. Lear terrifies because in one sense, it says too much. Its metaphysical implications overwhelm its strictly domestic conflicts, and the great problem is how to transcend the narrative and arrive in that truly transcendental last third of the play; into an area where even Shakespeare trod only once.

With Macbeth, the fear is different. Unlike Lear which uses natural imagery to achieve cosmic proportions or Hamlet which weaves endless ambiguities, Macbeth is a plot; a series of inescapably chronological incidents which defy reshuffling or reduction. To play Macbeth is to embroil oneself in the mechanics of that murder-mystery, that detective-thriller, that horror-story which is the play. To the extent that Macbeth is ever 'successful', it succeeds the way a good Agatha Christie does. There is an atmosphere of dread, an overwhelming sense of menace, a series of crimes, pangs of conscience, fears of discovery, and a denouement which is as predictable as anything in pulp-fiction. To avoid this melodramatic inevitability, some directors go for what is sometimes called 'the Christian parable'. In this dispensation, Macbeth is seen as a battleground for forces of good and evil. Macbeth himself becomes a kind of bellicose Faustus; Lady Macbeth, a female Mephistophilis; Duncan, a secular symbol for God, and the Witches, a triplicated version of the Evil Angel. Viewed this way, the play becomes a sermon on the inescapability of retribution and, using some magnificent wads of verse, a few heady battle-scenes and a 19th century interpretation of character, the play is made to trumpet out the highly original fact that crime doesn't pay.

Obviously, this kind of approach reduces the magnitude of the play, but more important, it is a common misinterpretation of what the play is patently about.

The tragedy of Macbeth lies not in his fate, but in his state.

An overwhelming evil pressure is brought to bear on
a simple, uncomplicated nature. A soldier, for whom
military slaughter is a way of life, is suddenly confronted
with the existential meaning of the act of murder. He is
now asked not to decimate a faceless enemy but to cut down
a single individual, and one who embodies all the authority
of the realm. It is like an up-and-coming infantry sergeant
being singled out to assassinate a head-of-state, or viewed
in terms of its historical magnitude, an ordinary mortal
prompted to the most outrageous crime imaginable: the
murder of God. For what is Duncan if not God; a king by
divine right, a regent who is the very embodiment of all
those Christian virtues which plead 'like angels trumpet-
tongue'd against his taking off'. The murder of such a king
is the supreme arrogance; the rewards of such a murder
much less significant than the frisson of committing such
an act. Macbeth murders not for kingship but to experience
the ecstasy of such an action. He doesn't really have to
be goaded very far. In his very first scene, his imagination
is already busy pre-figuring the crime. His 'thought'
' whose murder yet is but fantastical' , shakes so 'his
single state of man, that function is smother'd in surmise'.
But no sooner has the murderous implication been planted
by Lady Macbeth than his face becomes a book 'where men
may read strange matters'. Within the space of two scenes
his surmise is unsmother'd.

But how can a competent, hardworking, not-very-
imaginative officer summon up the magnitude demanded by
such an act? How can anyone as work-a-day and secure
as Macbeth consider so outrageous a leap? He cannot.
Nothing in the play suggests the enormity of such a con-
cealed ambition. Everything suggests the docile conformity
of the professional military-man. Left to himself, he
would be quite happy to soldier along secure in Duncan's
high esteem, gold-bricking his way to General and then
perhaps to some exalted staff-position where, far from
the broil of battle, he would slither into a comfortable
old age. If it were left to him, whatever ambition he
harboured would have loosed itself through conventional
channels. But it is not left to him for Macbeth - like the
thirteenth man at table or the poor sap who inadvertently
tramples the ju-ju of an evil genie, is chosen. The
diabolical powers who sometimes test their mettle by

arbitrarily selecting a mortal scapegoat, choose this simple, stout-hearted officer and make him the tool of diabolical intention.

Once he is chosen, everything in his world is subordinated to their design. The Captain's wife, a frustrated, unchilded (breastfeeding notwithstanding) woman for whom social-climbing and sexual domination are convenient compensations for orgasm and motherhood, is easily converted to their use. Her spirit is rife for invasion from without, and invaded she is, by the same coruscating forces which have singled out Macbeth for destruction. A remorseless voodooienne, the great-great-great-grandmother of a Marie Leveau, infiltrates her body as deftly as the spirit of the dead occupies the frame of a human being designated as a medium between the two wolrds, and subtly, invisibly, Lady Macbeth's own ambitions comingle with those of Hecate or Diana. Her familiars, three embodiments of Satan's will, tend upon her like the obedient disciples of a coven, and with all the magical rites available to the 'old religion', Macbeth is manipulated into murder and self-destruction. But Satan's old adversary throws up the usual obstacles; pangs of conscience produce delays; remorse prevents prompt completion. At every turn, Macbeth must be supported along his route lest the diabolical design be spoiled. He constantly turns to his wife for reassurance and absolution. He is too simple, too Christian, to suspect her complicity in that design, too unimaginative to realize he has been appropriated for devil's work. At the close of his life, still blind to the nature of his true state, he knows he must pay for his crimes - for murder and tyranny - but he never once suspects these have been fastened to him as surely as the amulets tied to the witch-doctor's chain. His modicum of self-knowledge extends only to the visible world. He knows he has made a mess of running the country; he has enough political sense to know Malcolm is plotting against him and that his crown is unsafe. He can visualize political enemies, but never that daemonic force methodically bringing about his ruin. Like a man ignorant of the disease which is steadily consuming him, Macbeth flails at his symptoms but never discovers their cause.

Highly fanciful, you may say. Or, if you're tolerantly-inclined, why not? We've had a Christian Macbeth; a

Gangster Macbeth; an Oriental Macbeth; a Primitive Macbeth; a Political Macbeth; why not a jinxed Macbeth?

The only reason 'why not' is if the material resists. Any interpretation of any so-called 'classic' is like an old whore yielding to a new client's embrace. If Shakespeare's 'old whore' resisted this particular embrace, there would be grounds for withdrawing gracefully or otherwise, but what impressed me working on the play in this frame-of-mind is that the 'old whore' lammed into it like nobody's business.

Take, for example, that mouldy old carbuncle on the old whore's arse. I refer to the Lady Macduff Scene. In this version, the three creatures who tend on Lady Macbeth, who serve and subvert the victim of the hex, take Macbeth's line 'To crown my thoughts with acts, Be it thought and done' and convert it according to their black-magical proclivities. The witches, using the homeopathic magic which is their stock-in-trade, don the costumes of Lady Macduff and child, and act out the murder that Macbeth has envisaged. In the world of black magic, it is possible to destroy an enemy by simulating his death. What Macbeth watches is the diabolical charade of the murder he wants to see committed and, according to this convention, it follows 'naturally' that Macduff learns his wife and children have been slain. Macbeth's 'fantastical thought' when not 'smother'd in surmise' is transmitted into reality. Which is to say, one reality supplants another, for diabolical intention devoutly held and fastidiously practised, unquestionably produces tangible results. For some cynical observers, this is almost a definition of history.

The first section of the play - from the imaginary murder of Duncan and Banquo to the meeting with Lady Macbeth is viewed here as a prophetic vision of everything that will befall Macbeth. A true prophetic vision contains, as does this opening collage, all the highpoints of a man's life circumscribed by the spirit which will eventually destroy him. In intention, it is like the stream of images which are supposed to pass through the mind of a man toppling to his death. If it is not played in that spirit and with that speed, it becomes a tedious index of the play's main events. If collage-playing has any essential corollaries, they are speed and definition. One without the other is useless.

The danger of any interpretation of a play by Shakespeare is the assumption - professed or implied - that one has hit upon the definitive meaning of the work. It is presumption of this kind which triggers off the hilarious disputes that scholars frequently indulge in. To avoid this footling jollity, I should say that, at this juncture of my life, influenced as I was by readings of voodoo and black magic in my high-school years, by the recent prominence of Polanski's Rosemary's Baby, by the certainty that any production of Macbeth that did not begin with an assimilation of the meaning of the witches was evasion, I hit upon this view of the play. If I were a Czech working in occupied Prague, I am sure I could not see the play in anything but political terms. If I were a devout Christian, it is quite likely I would be unable to see the play except as a moral parable. I don't contend that this is the only way of seeing Macbeth, but I will sidle towards presumptuousness this far: in tackling the play in terms of pre-Christian belief, in terms of spells and hexes, I have found a diabolical centre to the play which nothing will ever make me relinquish. The oft-remarked-upon affinities between Hecate and Lady Macbeth is not an accident. The vague sense of complicity between Lady Macbeth and the witches, their unanimity of purpose, is not an accident. The hallucinated world in which Macbeth seems most at home (look at him at any social point in the play and you see a fish out of water) is not an accident. The opposition of light and darkness between Duncan's world and Macbeth's is not an accident. The form of the play, a fable begun with a ritual scene of witchcraft and studded with similar scenes at every crucial point of the plot, is not an accident.

We tend to forget that in the 17th century, diabolism was not only more prevalent, but more potent. Devil-worship was not yet the 'superstitious nonsense' it has become today; and yet, if the murder of Sharon Tate by a diabolically obsessed sect of young boys and girls proves anything, it is that diabolism is too ingrained in our natures ever to be thoroughly routed out. So long as Christianity dominates our lives, its diabolical antithesis must figure in our psychology. And because it does, works like Macbeth which, in my opinion, grew out of a time when devilry was as natural as breathing (the Guy Fawkes gunpowder plot coincided with the writing of Macbeth and if ever proof of daemonic influence was needed, that provided it in abundance) are closer to the rituals of the 'old religion' than we tend to believe, and in restoring the play to its proper 'religious' setting, it begins to operate more organically - no matter what structural changes are made in such a restoration.

In London, less so in Germany, Lady Macbeth's see-through nightie attracted more attention than it deserved. There is nothing quite so tedious as an over-explained production-scheme, but perhaps a word or two on this subject might help producers ward off future attacks.

If one follows the course of Lady Macbeth through this version, one sees a voodooienne, served by three creatures; opposed by one (the First Witch), suffered by the other two and ultimately toppled by all, the First Witch (in the self-crowning ceremony in the Funeral Scene) assuming the mantle of authority. After the Witches have hexed their mistress and engendered the madness which ushers in her death, the original woman - freed of diabolical influence - is restored. That is, Lady Macbeth as woman and wife returns. To assert the frailty of that woman as opposed to the hauteur of the voodooienne, she appears in a costume which emphasizes her femininity; that is her human characteristics as opposed to her malevolent attributes. In the original production, the actress wore a high-necked cape and full-length dress. To contrast with this trussed-up appearance, she is in the Sleepwalking scene virtually naked. In that scene, she was vulnerable, helpless, solitary and female; in every other, guileful, possessed, possessive and sub-human. I don't say that is the only way to make that distinction, but it is one way.

It may be charged that I have excised all the political elements from Macbeth. If so, I accept whatever blame may be attached to such excision. But personally I am bored silly by all that 'bleeding country', 'See us crowned at Scone' bunkum in the play, and find the testing-scene between Malcolm and Macduff one of Shakespeare's more laboured naiveties. In fact, the political threat which agitates Macbeth in the last quarter of the play is still contained in the penultimate scene where I have tried to externalize the paranoia Macbeth experiences in being encircled by an invading army. But, one must remember, for a man who is the captive of demons, an insurgent army is not so much a revolutionary force attempting to establish a respectable monarchy as it is another spasm in his ultimate breakdown. And if I am taken to task for bringing Birnam Wood on to the stage in the form of witches' brooms, I would answer that a man in the final stages of hallucinatory breakdown may be allowed a glimpse of the forces that have conspired to destroy him. But more pertinent is the fact that what we see on stage is only a reflection of what Macbeth sees, and so all questions of reality have to be referred back to the psychotic protagonist through whose distorted vision we view the play.

EXERCISES

The more one goes through the motions of play-production, the more one realizes the inappropriateness of the conventional rehearsal process. What is the premise behind most rehearsals? Mainly, that in a limited period of time, actors are expected to learn a certain number of words and a certain number of moves in order to achieve a half-decent state-of-readiness before an audience. Even in Continental companies where the rehearsal-period is sometimes eight and twelve weeks, the additional time is spent polishing results usually achieved in three or four weeks' time. The essential requirement, and one would have thought the most obvious, has either been ignored or heedlessly taken for granted; namely, that actors have to undergo a certain number of pressures and impacts to make them ready to deliver the experience contained in their play. This may sound like walloping the obvious, but the one factor missing from most rehearsal-periods is precisely that of experience, i.e. the living-through of those tensions and revelations which charge characters with emotions and endow them with insights. The 'experience' of most rehearsal-periods is what actors usually refer to as "getting the technical things straight"; the memorization of words, the mapping-out of moves, the assimilation of props and costume. One does not underestimate these 'technical' needs by pointing out that in preparing to convey something of the shape and feel of life, one needs more than the mechanistic fluency of its surface. Nor am I proposing an endless period of depth-analysis a la Stanislavsky - although time could be worse spent - what I am saying is that the richness of the experience delivered in performance is in direct ratio to the experience undergone in preparation. It is too easily forgotten that the surest factor in any production is the text which has been furnished from the outset. The most difficult requisite is the sub-textual physiology that qualifies actors to speak the text; that brings them to that state of artistic maturity which makes certain manifestations inevitable. Which is why, for instance, in rehearsing The Hostage, Joan Littlewood was right to deny her actors any knowledge of what Brendan Behan had written and instead, had them march around the barred roof of her theatre inculcating the experience of regimentation. And why Grotowsky, to cite an even more convincing example, spends most of his preparation-period in exploring the archetypal underbelly of his play leaving sound (words or musical expressions of same) to the very last.

The first stage of any rehearsal-period should introduce actors to the forms and images they will subsequently discover working on the play. By exposing them to naked physical syntax, they are given the means with which they will eventually construct the action-language of the production.
    To the best of my knowledge, these are original exercises, devised by myself for use with The Open Space Company, but like all scientific inventions, I would not be surprised to learn that variations are being used in Prague, Paris, Zagreb and Canarsie.

Warm-Up

Actors in pairs using subtle hand-and-finger signals try to match up each other's movements. The face is kept expressionless. All emotional attitudes are conveyed by means of the hand-and-finger movements. The acting-partner, face expressionless, also using only hands and fingers, reacts.

Adjustments

One actor is seated at a table. He is utterly neutral - without character, situation or intention. A second actor enters the scene and, by playing his chosen character, situation and intention, automatically transforms the first actor into a relevant partner. The first actor, as quickly as possible, adapts to the situation imposed on him by the second actor. Before the scene is allowed to finish, a third actor enters (this being the cue for the first actor's exit) and, playing an entirely different situation forces the second actor to adjust to a completely new set of circumstances. Etc. etc. etc. The most delicate point of contact - apart from the obvious adjustment of first actor to second, is the moment the third actor intrudes on the scene already in progress between actors 1 and 2. If the rhythm of the exercise is right, there is a split-second cut (without pause) between the entrance of actor 3 and the exit of actor 1. So that scenes never actually finish but unexpectedly dissolve into new ones.

The acting-exercise is the greatest challenge an actor has; greater even than the demands of a role. Using a flexible form which accommodates improvisation and physical invention, he is asked to conjure up something telling and creative. Very often, the exercise is devoid of any substance except that which he brings to it. A role, no matter how large or small, gives the actor some kind of framework and textual base. No matter how feeble his own personal contribution, there is always some given content to fall back on. The exercise is an invitation to unveil himself completely; to dazzle and overwhelm using his own personal stock of imagery, his own innate style, his own peculiar brand of genius. It lays bare his talent - which is why it is such a terrifying act.

The Clothesline

A well-known line from Shakespeare is chosen, i.e. 'If it were done when 'tis done t'were well it were done quickly' or 'Is this a dagger I see before me, the handle toward my hand' etc. etc.

The Company is placed in a circle. Each actor is given one word of the line.
1. The first actor begins a definite 'reading' of the line - using only the first word of the line. The second actor (on his right) attempts to pick up the colour of that line-reading and continue it on his word. The other actors, in their turn, do likewise. If successful, once the line has rippled through the entire company, it has been given a definite and comprehensible group-rendering. When unsuccessful, each actor will have

simply mimicked the attitude of the first, and the result is a slightly-modified repetition of one emotional colour. A good test is to re-play the line to see if it would pass muster in any sort of interpretation of the speech. If the line has been successfully rendered, it should then be reversed - with the actor holding the last word playing out the final colour (as he ended) and everyone else obliged to recreate their original word-reading.

2. The same line is played out without emotional consistency. Each actor is obliged to choose an emotional colour as far removed as possible from the one preceding him.

3. The same line is played out with an extravagant, non-naturalistic physical action. A gesture or movement is selected - in a split second - which has no relation whatsoever to the one preceding. There should be no seconds allowed for preparation, the choice being made almost involuntarily.

4. The same line is played out with an attempt at consistent physical action. The first actor makes the first motion of a gesture. Each actor in turn is obliged to fulfil the natural tendency of that gesture. Here too, there is the danger of mimicry; that each actor will only perform a slightly varied version of the first gesture instead of allowing it to graduate naturally.

5. The Shakespearian line is put to a familiar tune. In this variation, the first actor is allowed three or four words so that the gist of the melodic line can be recognized; the object then being for the melody to be continued - without break - from one to the other. (The bugaboo of this exercise is the unequal musical knowledge of any given company; what is an 'old standard' for one actor is totally unknown to another. It is best to stick to songs with a popular national character or indisputable standards like 'Happy Birthday To You' and 'Silent Night'.

6. The line is played out in a stock accent: Irish, Scots, Brooklynese, Yiddish, etc. The first actor has only one word with which to establish the accent. Again, one should try for some kind of dramatic variety in the line so as to avoid the tendency for each actor

merely displaying their version of Scots, Irish, Yiddish, etc.
7. The line is then played out only in physical movements. The aim of the group-movement should be to unify the emotional colouring of the line - (as with 1.) The same pitfalls of mimicry and imitation should be avoided. The physical action of each actor should be as precise and fragmented as the words were in Exercise 1.

In all of these variations, the prime requisite is the unbroken continuity of the exercise. If there are preparational gaps between words, or if the line loses the fluency of a natural speech rhythm, it is a failure. It is easy for these exercises to dwindle into isolated party-pieces which, of course, destroys the collective purpose for which they have been devised.

Death Circle

The actors form a circle and begin intoning any prayer of their own choice. The circle moves around the perimeter of the room. At some point on that perimeter, a white mark has been painted. On a signal, the praying and circling stops abruptly. Whoever has reached the white mark is obliged to die in some way of his own choosing. The rhythm, style and manner of his death is entirely up to the actor - hence it can be straight, comic, abrupt, elongated or whatever. No two actors may perform the same death. The dead actor remains on the floor until the entire group dies.

Howdown

The company forms a circle. A leader is selected, and he or she begins to clap out a rhythm which the others quickly duplicate, syncopate and embellish. An actor steps into the centre of the circle and begins performing a speech from the play - adjusting the rhythm of his delivery to the tempo of the group's clapping. As the clapping tempo changes (and the changes should not simply go from fast to slow, but contain differences of volume, texture, and dramatic character), the actor changes his speech accordingly. As soon as he feels he has had enough, without interruption, he resumes his place in the circle cueing another actor into his place in the centre. Throughout the exercise, the object is for the actor to perform the group will. His interpretation is entirely regulated by the changes occurring in the tempi of the group. Eventually, the leader can be forsaken altogether, and the group should be able to ring its changes by itself. When this can be brought about smoothly, it indicates a highly-developed sense of group-contact.

Macbeth Stew

Different scenes from the play are divided between five couples. The scenes should be short, compact and, wherever possible, self-sufficient, i.e. the Malcolm-Macduff Scene (IV.3), the Conspiracy Scene between Macbeth and Lady Macbeth (I.7), Banquo and Macbeth (III.1) etc. Since several scenes may include Macbeth, he should be played by as many different actors as is feasible.
1. The scenes are played out straight.
2. The scenes are conditioned by unrelated physical actions (i.e. Macbeth and Lady Macbeth playing tennis, taking ballet instructions, doing the dishes, etc. with the scene's original intentions observed as faithfully as possible.
3. The scenes, with unrelated physical business, are played so that that intentions are radically changed; changed, that is, in accordance with the dictates of the new business (i.e. Macbeth petulant at having to wash while Lady M. dries; Lady Macbeth irritated by Macbeth's ineptitude at ballet-instructions, etc. etc.
4. On a signal, the couples playing their scenes simultaneously, split up and begin playing their scenes with other characters. Now a Lady Macbeth may be playing her Conspiracy Scene with a Macduff who is playing his Testing Scene. The more dominant physical action dominates the scene, and the words become nothing more

than a sound-cover for sub-textual meanings wholly unrelated to the text, i.e. (Macduff, still using the words of his original scene, may be playing the hen-pecked husband of a domineering wife; Macduff, using his original text, may be urged to murder by a shrewish Lady Macbeth, etc.)
5. Signals are then given in quick succession with only one or two minutes pause between. On each signal, characters break away from their original partners, and quickly match up with another; any other. As they do so, their scene automatically changes its action, attitude and intention. In every case, the more dominant idea should be allowed to prevail; the playing-partner adapting as quickly as possible.

The reason for fracturing a Shakespearian scene - altering the original meaning of its text but keeping the words intact, complicating its situation with incongruous business and unrelated acting-partners, is to compel actors to control both disparate and multiple elements. One part of the actor's technique is dealing with words, another with feelings, a third with actions, a fourth with contact, and all the while, all these elements are shifting, changing, reversing, returning. The overall effect, from the audience's standpoint, is simultaneity, but within this jumble of words and actions, the actor is the regulator of a highly sophisticated piece of equipment: himself. Therefore, jumbled as it certainly is, it is never unaccountable chaos; unless of course, the actor sinks beneath the multiple pressures. When successful, it is a rich fusion of several elements which, like the components of a printing-press, create an impression of impossible complexity, and yet, when the printing-press slows down, are individually recognizable.

These kinds of exercises deal with the actor as mechanism because the human being which animates the actor is a mechanism; just as theatre is the synthesis of many mechanisms. The danger is that the performance of these mechanisms produces a purely mechanistic effect - which of course has nothing to do with the intentions of art. In such a case, it would be as if the complicated machinery of the printing-press was functioning only to demonstrate the facility of its equipment, without actually printing

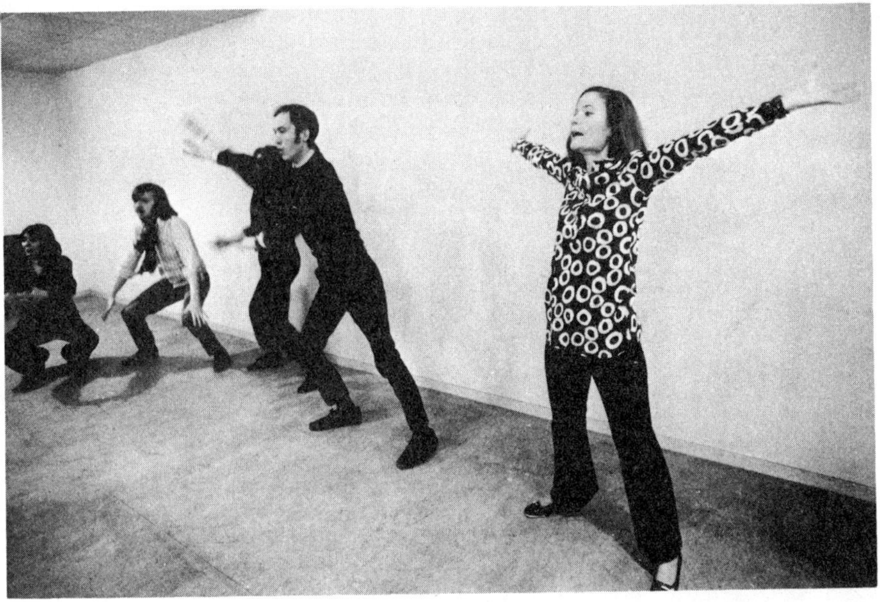

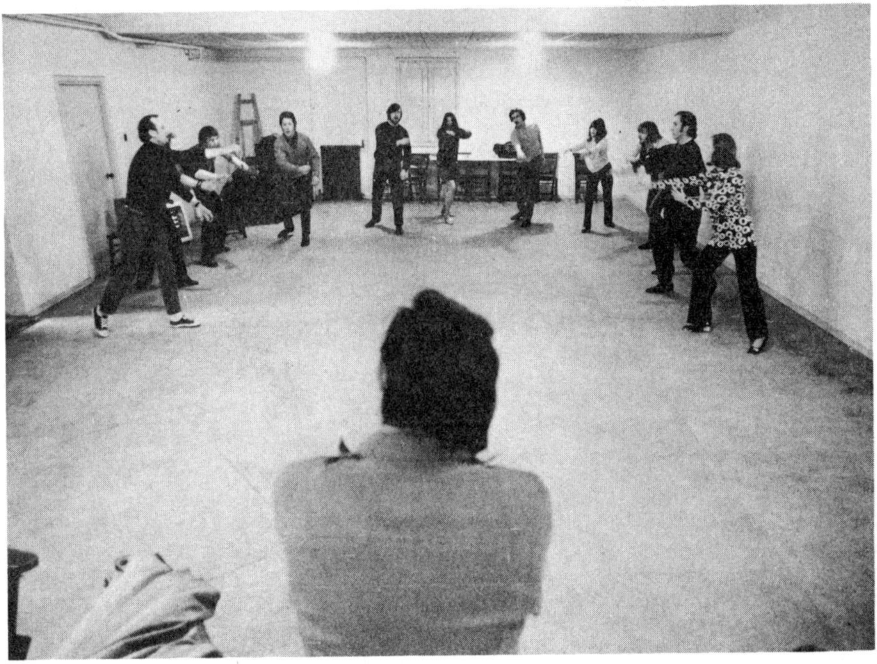

anything. It is important that the end for which these mechanisms are being lubricated is always kept in mind; so that exercises never lose themselves in displays of technique, but utilise technique to express more than could be expressed if technique were not that highly sophisticated.

The actor who complains he is being treated like a robot is often bawling for the self-indulgence of the monocelled performer. Give me my lines and my moves, cries his sub-text, and I will give you a thundering exhibition of my immovable cliches. If there were no other benefit to these exercises, it would be sufficient that they rob the actor of the complacency which type-casting and artistic sloth engender in his being. The actor is always asking for a 'challenge' until he actually gets one; then you realize what he meant was a big, showy part for himself.

Male-Female

A male actor chooses a typical female situation (i.e. instruction on childbirth, trying on lingerie, receiving beauty-parlour treatment) and plays it out in his own character but with all the appropriate female choices. There should be no attempt at phoney-female voices or female-parody. The object of the exercise is for the male to assimilate the female situation as faithfully as possible in his own character.

Multiples

Best performed with a group of twelve. All standing in a circle.

1ST ACTOR. Lays down a basic rhythmic beat (not a melody) which serves as a bass-accompaniment to the exercise.

2ND ACTOR. Augments this beat with a rhythm of his own which, in range and texture, is as dissimilar as possible but still fits into the given rhythm.

3RD ACTOR. Does likewise.

4TH ACTOR. Does likewise.

5TH ACTOR. Chooses the name of a disease and performs that rhythmically, i.e. 'laryngitis' - broken down into sound-components: lah-ryn-gi-tis, lah-ryn-gi-tis, lah-ryn-gi-tis, etc. etc.

6TH ACTOR. Continually repeats four bars of a popular song.

7TH ACTOR. Plays out an advertising slogan augmenting the group-rhythm: 'Daz Washes Whiter', 'Guinness is Good For You', 'Keep Britain Tidy' etc. etc.

8TH ACTOR. Punctuates group-rhythm with a cry. No matter how searing the cry, it must - in some way - fit into the collective rhythm and must never be rhythmically arbitrary.

9TH ACTOR. Using only plosives, non-vocalized sounds, adds to the collective rhythm.

10TH ACTOR. Using his body as an instrument, claps out a beat which fits into the collective rhythm.

11TH ACTOR. Using sharp, rhythmic gestures, adds movements that fit into the collective rhythm.

12TH ACTOR. Begins to tell the story of his life in a dry, matter-of-fact, conventional style.

N.B. The group-rhythm must never be imitative but always complimentary; that is, everyone's contribution, by being tonally or texturally different from what has gone before, must enrich the overall texture of the whole.

Once the group-rhythm is under way, the director uses the Biographist (12th Actor) as a soloist, relegating everyone else to the level of accompaniment. He conducts the Biographist to the centre and signals for the background-

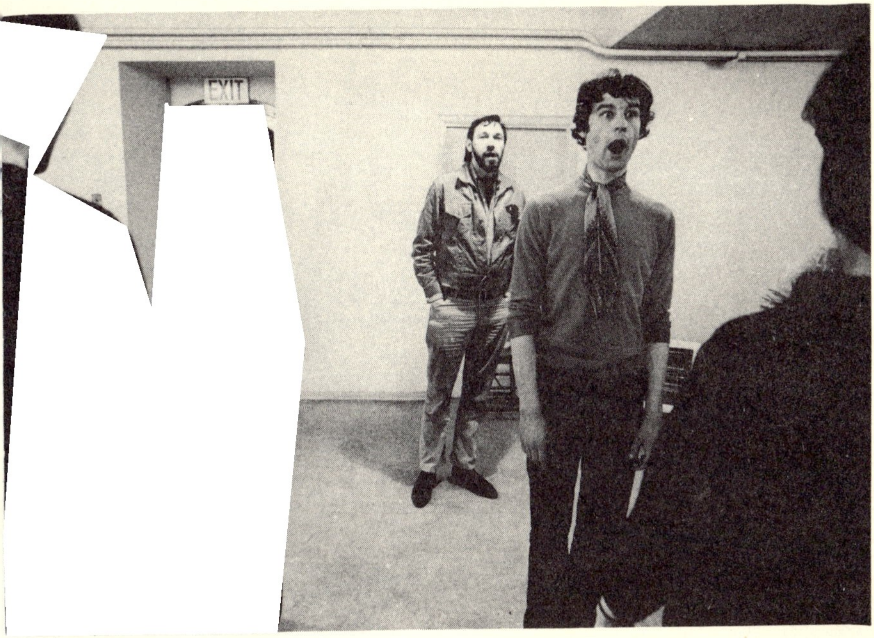
EXIT

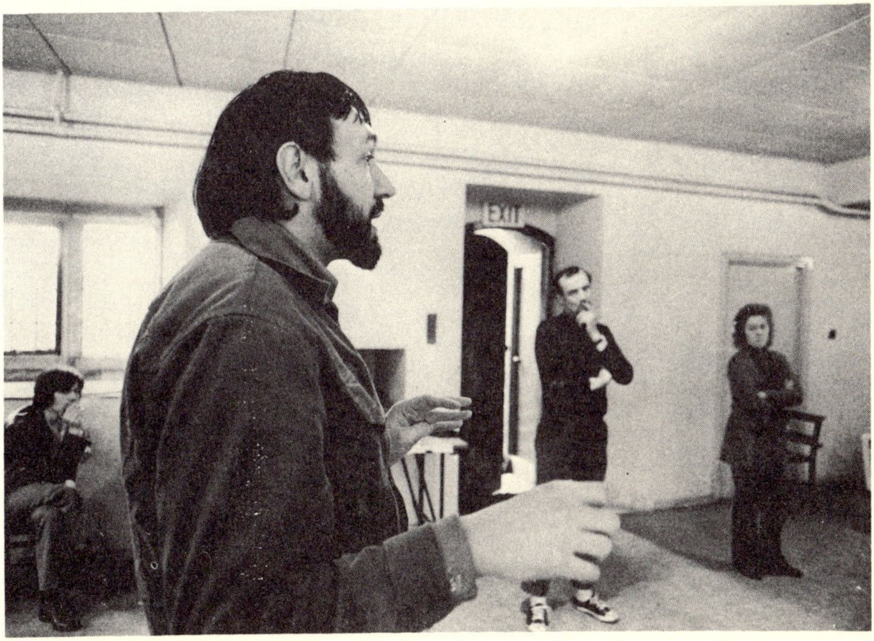
EXIT

actors to subside in volume. In this way, the soloist's biography becomes the main-line of the exercise; the others providing a dulled, but discernible, repeated accompaniment. Ideally, they are listening to the soloist while performing their own repeated contributions. Then the conductor (director) signals to another actor to become the Biographist -soloist. The new Biographist abandons his own rhythmic contribution and begins telling the story of his life while the previous Biographist (12th Actor) retires to the background still speaking his biography, but now as part of the dulled accompaniment. This process continues until all have become Biographists. (During the soloist's performance, the director-conductor regulates the group's performance as he wishes - changing tempi and dynamics).

Towards the end of the exercise, soloists, instead of being waved into the background, remain in the centre telling their stories while other soloists are signalled in. Eventually, there are four or five biographies being spoken simultaneously; then eight, nine, ten, etc. Eventually, everyone is speaking their biography at the same time. Again, the din is a concentration factor, and the object is to retain the line of one's own story in the midst of the jumble-of-speech on every side.

Help Play

The room is littered with numerous obstacles; overturned chairs, banana-peels, balls, heavy equipment, trays of water, etc. One set of actors (the Movers) are blindfolded; alongside them a second set of actors (the Helpers). The Helpers' job is to guide the Movers from one end of the room to the other without colliding against any of the obstacles. This is done by the Helpers whispering instructions into the ears of the Movers. If there are six or seven people performing the exercise at the same time, the din of everyone talking at once is a useful complicating factor encouraging greater concentration. Once the Movers have successfully traversed the room, they become the Helpers and vice versa.

In preparing this version of Macbeth, there are three acting priorities.

1. The company has to mesh together so perfectly that sub-textual meaning registers as strongly as text and, (another way of putting the same idea), that familiar text - which is what Macbeth is - does not override the new emphases and nuances projected through it.
2. That resources are opened for the actor with which he can transcend the conventional means of performing Shakespearian language- so that, for instance, when the spirit moves him, he can create a sound, a movement, a gesture or a cry which is dramatically appropriate and still connected to the literary framework from which it springs.
3. That personal conceptions of the play's meaning are able to find original modes of expression which reinforce the production's meaning, and do not tumble into that ever-open pit of 'stylistic jazziness' which tempts the actor into flashy novelties which are subsequently rationalized as 'originality'.

Postscript Any scene from this version of the play which could occur just as easily in a conventional production of Shakespeare's Macbeth must be stylistically incorrect.

A MACBETH

A MACBETH was commissioned by the Hessisches
Staadstheater of Wiesbaden which presented it at the May
Festival of 1969. It subsequently played at The Open
Space Theatre in London and toured Italy and France. The
original cast was as follows:

MACBETH	Nikolas Simmonds
2ND MACBETH	Peter Marinker
3RD MACBETH	Jon Croft
LADY MACBETH	Thelma Holt
1ST WITCH	Louise Breslin
2ND WITCH	Jennifer Armitage
3RD WITCH	Lesley Ward
DUNCAN	Gordon Whiting
BANQUO	Robert Ashley
MACDUFF	Robin McGee
MALCOLM	Ralph Arliss

The play was designed by John Napier and directed
by Charles Marowitz.

(Lights come up on effigy of Macbeth. In front of it, back to audience, stands LADY MACBETH. On a signal, the three WITCHES enter and surround the effigy. Each adds bits to it until it clearly resembles MACBETH. After a pause, LADY MACBETH begins to intone an incantation)

LADY MACBETH.
    I'll drain him dry as hay
    Sleep shall neither night nor day
    Hang upon his penthouse lid.
    He shall live a man forbid.
    Weary seven-nights nine-times-nine
    Shall he dwindle, peak and pine.

(One of the WITCHES hands LADY MACBETH a smoking poker. With it, she slowly obliterates the wax eyes of the effigy. The lights fade)

(Lights up. Enter DUNCAN, BANQUO, MALCOLM and MACDUFF. The stage is filled with a pleasant, summery glow. Birds are chirping in background)

KING.
    This castle hath a pleasant seat; the air
    Nimbly and sweetly recommends itself
    Unto our gentle senses.

BANQUO.
    This guest of summer,
    The temple-haunting martlet, does approve
    By his loved mansionry that the heaven's breath

      Smells wooingly here; no jutty, frieze,
      Buttress, nor coign of vantage, but this bird
      Hath made his pendent bed and procreant cradle;
      Where they most breed and haunt I have observed
      The air is delicate.

      (Enter LADY MACBETH)

KING.
      See, see, our honoured hostess -
      The love that follows us sometimes is our trouble,
      Which still we thank as love. Herein I teach you
      How you shall bid 'God 'ield us' for your pains,
      And thank us for your trouble.

LADY MACBETH.
      All our service
      In every point twice done and then done double
      Were poor and single business to contend
      Against those honours deep and broad wherewith
      Your majesty loads our house. For those of old,
      And the late dignities heaped up to them,
      We rest your hermits.

KING.
      Where is the Thane of Cawdor?
      We coursed him at the heels and had a purpose
      To be his purveyor; but he rides well,
      And his great love, sharp as his spur, hath holp him
      To his home before us.
      Fair and noble hostess,
      We are your guest tonight.

LADY MACBETH.
      Your servants ever
      Have theirs, themselves, and what is theirs, in compt,
      To make their audit at your highness' pleasure,
      Still to return your own.

KING.
      Give me your hand;
      Conduct me to mine host. We love him highly,
      And shall continue our graces towards him.

(Others pass through door, but as DUNCAN and
BANQUO are about to enter, MACBETH suddenly
appears. He stabs DUNCAN. LADY MACBETH stabs
BANQUO. WITCHES quickly spirit away DUNCAN,
BANQUO and LADY MACBETH. Blackout)

(Lights up. MACBETH surrounded by MACBETHS 1
& 2 dash downstage together and begin the next.
MACBETHS 1 & 2 whisper the words MACBETH
speaks)

MACBETH. (breathlessly)
    If it were done when 'tis done, then 'twere well
    It were done quickly. If the assassination
    Could trammel up the consequence, and catch
    With his surcease success - that but this blow
    Might be the be-all and the end-all! - here,
    But here, upon this bank and shoal of time,
    We'd jump the life to come. But in these cases
    We still have judgement here - that we but teach
    Bloody instructions, which, being taught, return
    To plague the inventor. This even-handed justice
    Commends the ingredience of our poisoned chalice
    To our own lips. (Turning quickly - to LADY M)
    He's here in double trust.

LADY MACBETH.
    Was the hope drunk
    Wherein you dress'd yourself. Hath it slept since?
    And wakes it now to look so green and pale?

MACBETH.
    I am his kinsman and his subject
    Strong both against the deed.

LADY MACBETH.
    Wouldst thou be afear'd
    To be the same in thine own act and valour
    As thou art in desire?

MACBETH.
    His virtues
    Will plead like angels, trumpet-tongue'd against

The deep damnation of his taking-off.

LADY MACBETH.
Wouldst thou have that
Which thou esteem'st the ornament of life,
And live a coward in thine own esteem?
Letting 'I dare not' wait upon 'I would'
Like the poor cat in the adage.

(Cut to:)

DUNCAN.
I have begun to plant thee and will labour
To make thee full of growing.

MACBETH. (kneeling)
The service and the loyalty I owe
In doing it, pays itself.

LADY MACBETH.
From this time
Such I account thy love.

DUNCAN.
More is thy due than more than all can pay.

MACBETH. (back with LADY MACBETH)
He hath honour'd me of late, and I have bought
Golden opinions from all sorts of people...

DUNCAN. (to Banquo)
No more that Thane of Cawdor shall deceive
Our bosom interest. Go pronounce his present death.

MACBETH.
I should against his murderer shut the door
Not bear the knife myself.

LADY MACBETH.
The sleeping and the dead
Are but as pictures: tis the eye of childhood
That fears a painted devil.

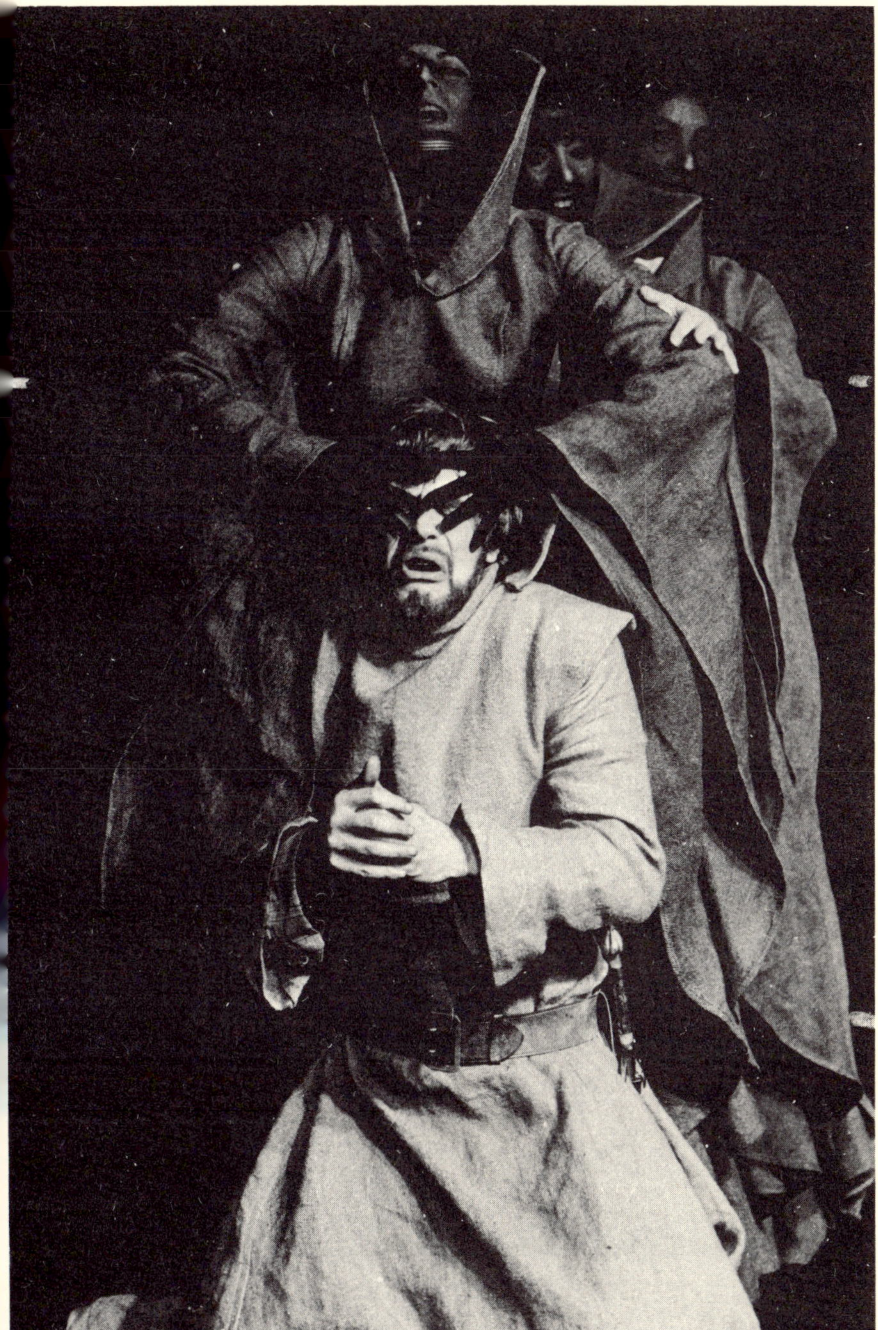

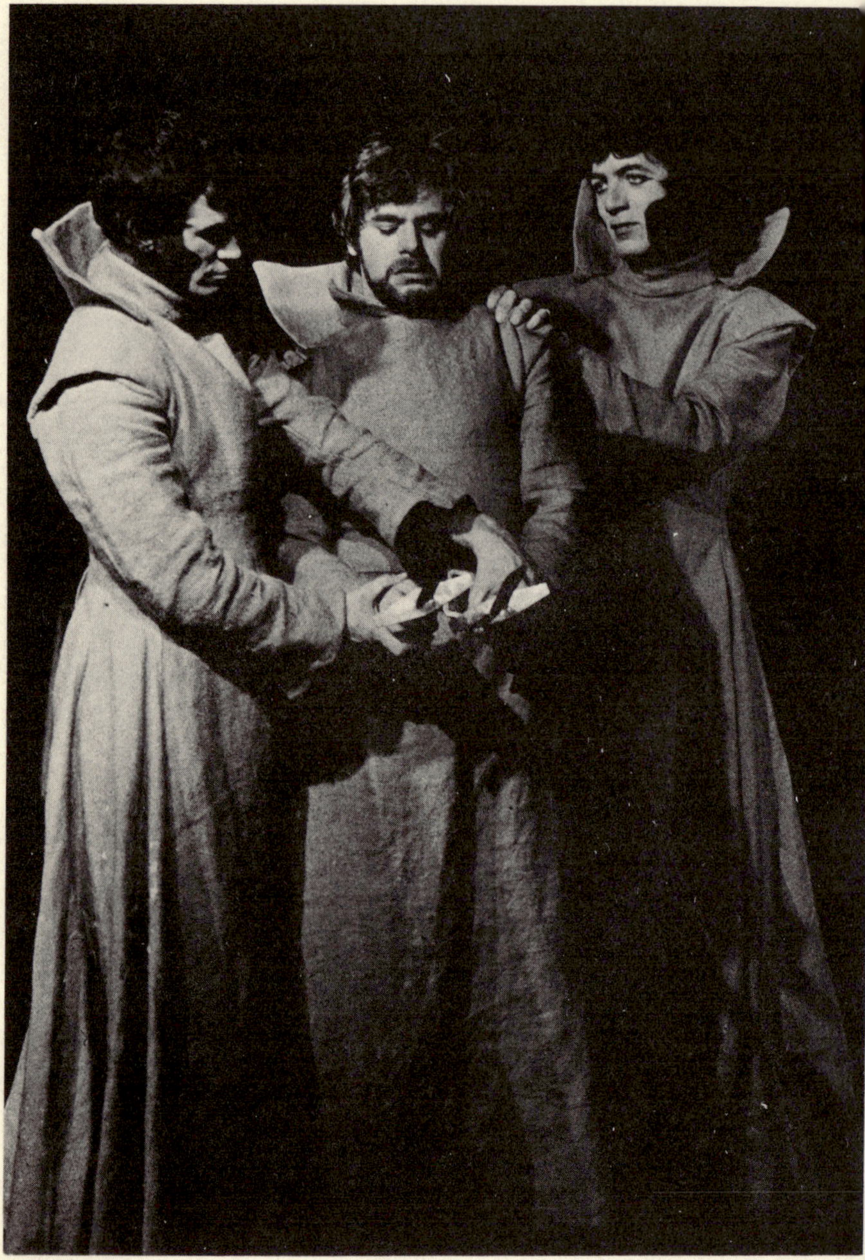

MACBETH.
    We will proceed no further in this business.

LADY MACBETH.
    Thou shalt be what thou art promis'd.

    (Cut to:)

BANQUO.
    You shall be king.

1ST WITCH.
    And Thane of Cawdor too.

MACBETH. (to WITCH)
    The Thane of Cawdor lives; a prosperous gentleman.

1ST WITCH.
    Go pronounce his present death.

2ND WITCH.
    And with his former title greet Macbeth.

MACBETH.
    Why do you dress me in borrowed robes?

WITCHES.
    Hail to thee, Thane of Glamis
                Thane of Cawdor,
    All hail Macbeth.

LADY MACBETH.
    That shalt be king hereafter.

MACBETH.
    To be king.
    Stands not within prospect of belief
    More than...

DUNCAN.
    Is execution done on Cawdor?

MACBETH. (limply)
> To be Cawdor.

DUNCAN. (to BANQUO)
> There's no art
> To find the mind's construction in the face.
> He was a gentleman on whom I built
> An absolute trust.

MACBETH. (to LADY MACBETH)
> Prithee peace:
> I dare do all that may become a man
> Who dares do more is none.

2ND MACBETH.
> What beast was't then
> That made you break this enterprise to me?
> When you durst do it, then you were a man,
> And to be more than what you were, you should
> Be so much more the man.

> (Pause)

DUNCAN.
> Look how our partner's rapt?

LADY MACBETH.
> Are you a man?

MACBETH. (fiercely)
> Ay, and a bold one.

LADY MACBETH.
> Ay, in the catalogue ye go for men
> As hounds and greyhounds, mongrels, spaniels, curs,
> Shoughs, water-rugs and demi-wolves are clept
> All by the name of dogs.

BANQUO.
> I dreamt last night of the three weird sisters.
> To you they have showed some truth.

MACBETH. (to BANQUO)
>I think not of them.
>>(to LADY MACBETH)
>We will proceed no further in this business.

LADY MACBETH.
>I have given suck and know
>How tender 'tis to love the babe that milks me.
>I would, while it was smiling in my face,
>Have pluck'd my nipple from his boneless gums
>And dash'd the brains out had I so sworn.

MACBETH.
>Prithee peace.

BANQUO.
>Good sir, why do you start and seem to fear
>Things that do sound so fair?

WITCHES. (overlapping BANQUO's last word)
>Is foul and foul is fair
>Glamis - Cawdor - King - All.

MACBETH. (to himself)
>This supernatural soliciting
>Cannot be ill, cannot be good.
>If ill,
>Why hath it given me earnest of success
>Commencing in a truth? I am Thane of Cawdor.

WITCHES.
>And shalt be King hereafter!

2ND MACBETH.
>Oftentimes, to win us to our harm
>The instruments of darkness tell us truths;

3RD MACBETH.
>Win us with honest trifles, to betray's
>In deepest consequence.

>(MACBETH, considering this, turns suspiciously to LADY MACBETH)

LADY MACBETH. (nonchalantly)
    So foul and fair a day I have not seen.

MACBETH. (hotly, to WITCHES)
    Say from whence
    You owe this strange intelligence;
    Speak, I charge you!

LADY MACBETH. (calming him; taking him round)
    Hie thee hither
    That I may pour my spirits in thine ear
    And chastize with the valour of my tongue
    All that impedes thee from the golden round
    Which fate and metaphysical aid doth seem
    To have thee crowned withal.

    (Led by LADY MACBETH and WITCHES into a circle)

3RD WITCH.
    Look what I have.

2ND WITCH.
    Show me, show me.

3RD WITCH. (grabbing MACBETH's thumb)
    Here I have a pilot's thumb
    Wracked as homeward he did come.

    (Places MACBETH's hand onto his sword)

WITCHES.
    A drum! A drum!
    Macbeth doth come.

    (While this is chanted, the WITCHES beat a tattoo on their sides. It is repeated until MACBETH is crowned in a mock-coronation ceremony)

1ST WITCH.
    Hail to thee Thane of Glamis.

2ND WITCH.
    Hail to thee, Thane of Cawdor.

3RD WITCH.
    All Hail Macbeth.

LADY MACBETH. (kneeling before him)
    That shalt be king hereafter.

MACBETH. (breaking ceremony, to LADY MACBETH)
    If we should fail.

LADY MACBETH.
    We fail.

2ND MACBETH. (rallying him)
    But screw your courage to the sticking place

3RD MACBETH.
    And we'll not fail.

DUNCAN. (insistently)
    Is execution done on Cawdor?

MACBETH. (defensively)
    The Thane of Cawdor lives.

WITCH.
    And shalt be king hereafter.

BANQUO.
    If you can look into the seeds of time
    And say which grain will grow
    And which will not.
    Speak then to me who neither beg nor fear
    Your favours nor your hate.

WITCHES. (by-passing MACBETH perform crowning
        ceremony on BANQUO)
    Hail, hail, hail.
    Lesser than Macbeth, yet much happier.

1ST WITCH.
    Thou shalt get kings, though thou be none.

MACBETH.
    No son of mine succeeding?

WITCHES.
    All hail, Banquo.

MACBETH.
    The seeds of Banquo, kings?

2ND WITCH.
    Lesser than Macbeth...

MACBETH.
    A fruitless crown...

3RD WITCH.
    Yet much happier...

MACBETH.
    A barren sceptre?

DUNCAN. (with BANQUO)
    Noble Banquo
    That hast no less deserv'd, nor must be known
    No less to have done so, let me enfold thee
    And hold thee to my heart.

MACBETH.
    For Banquo's issue have I filed my mind.

DUNCAN. (to MACBETH, agreeing)
    True, worthy Banquo.

MACBETH.
    For them the gracious Duncan have I murdered?

BANQUO. (holding out hand)
    It will be rain tonight.

2ND MACBETH.)
3RD MACBETH.)
    Then let it come down.

    (MACBETH issues signal; BANQUO dies. MACBETHS
    2 and 3 remove the static figure of BANQUO as if it
    were a store-dummy)

MACBETH. (to WITCHES)
    Shall Banquo's issue ever
    Reign in this kingdom?

1ST WITCH.
    Be bloody,

2ND WITCH.
    bold,

3RD WITCH.
    and resolute;

1ST WITCH.
    Laugh to scorn the power of man
    For none of woman born
    Shall harm Macbeth.

MACBETH.
    Shall Banquo's issue ever reign...

WITCH.)
WITCH.)
    Macbeth shall never vanquished be until
    Great Birnam Wood to High Dunsinane Hill
    Shall come against him.

MACBETH.
    That will never be.

LADY MACBETH.
    Then come,
    bend up each corporal agent to this terrible feat.
    Spurn fate...

MALCOLM. (building in volume)
> Bloody, luxurious, avaricious...

LADY MACBETH.
> Scorn death.

MALCOLM.
> False, deceitful, sudden malicious...

LADY MACBETH.
> Bear your hopes 'bove wisdom, grace and fear.

MALCOLM.
> Smacking of every sin that hath a name.
> (turns to MACBETH)
> If such a one be fit to govern, speak.

MACBETH. (lamely to MALCOLM)
> The spirits that know all mortal consequences
> Have pronounced me thus:
> Fear not Macbeth; for none of woman born

WITCHES. (whispering with MACBETH)
> Shall ere have power upon thee.

MALCOLM.
> God above deal between thee and me
> When I shall tread upon this tyrant's head
> Or wear it in my sword.

LADY MACBETH. (brazenly goading MACBETH)
> What's the boy Malcolm?

MALCOLM. (to LADY MACBETH imperiously)
> The son of Duncan
> From whom this tyrant holds the due of birth
> Which we now claim as ours.

MACBETH.
> Were I from Dunsinane away and clear
> Profit again should hardly draw me here.

LADY MACBETH.
> O proper stuff!
> Wouldst thou live a coward...
> To kiss the ground before Malcolm's feet
> And to be baited with the rabble's curse?

MACBETH. (surveying all)
> I dare do all that may become a man.

MACDUFF. (to other MACBETHS)
> Wife?

2ND MACBETH.
> Aye.

MACDUFF.
> Children?

3RD MACBETH.
> Aye.

MACDUFF.
> Servants, all?

2ND MACBETH.
> Aye.

MACDUFF. (to MACBETH)
> Turn hellhound, turn!
> Thou bloodier villain
> Than terms can give thee out.

BANQUO (turning on him)
> O Horror, horror, horror!
> Tongue nor heart cannot conceive or name thee.

MALCOLM.
> Not in the legions of horrid hell can come
> A devil more damned in evil.

DUNCAN. (turning on him)
> Speak if you can. What are you?

(MACBETH hemmed in by DUNCAN, BANQUO and
MACDUFF, backs away towards WITCHES)

WITCHES.
By the pricking of my thumbs
Something wicked this way comes.

MACBETH.
I bear a charmed life which must not yield
To one of woman born.

WITCHES. (with tattoo, as before)
A drum! A drum!
Macbeth doth come.

MACBETH.
Macbeth shall never vanquished be until
Great Birnam Wood to high Dunsinane Hill
Shall come against him.

(All circle MACBETH, LADY MACBETH, with effigy,
spell-casting in Background)

WITCHES.
A drum. A drum.
Macbeth doth come.

MACBETH.
I bear a charmed life...

WITCHES.
A drum. A drum.
Macbeth doth come.

(MACBETH is subdued. Cry. Blackout)

BANQUO. (As in the scene after the WITCHES'
disappearance)
The earth hath bubbles as the water has,
And these are of them. Whither are they vanished?

MACBETH.
Into the air; and what seemed corporal

Melted, as breath into the wind.

BANQUO.
Were such things here as we do speak about?
Or have we eaten on the insane root
That takes the reason prisoner?

MACBETH.
Your children shall be kings.

BANQUO.
You shall be king.

MACBETH.
And Thane of Cawdor too, went it not so?

BANQUO.
To the self same tune and words.
Hail King of Scotland, for so thou art.

MACBETH.
Hail root and father of many kings, for so thou art.

BANQUO.
Who's here?

2ND MACBETH. (entering)
The King hath happily received, Macbeth,
The news of thy success; and when he reads
Thy personal venture in the rebels' fight
His wonders and his praises do contend
Which should be thine, or his,
And, for an earnest of a greater honour,
He bade me from him call thee Thane of Cawdor
In which addition, hail, most worthy thane,
For it is thine.
(kneels)

WITCHES. (off)
All hail Thane of Cawdor.

BANQUO.
What! Can the devil speak true?

MACBETH.
> The Thane of Cawdor lives, a prosperous gentleman.
> Why do you dress me in borrowed robes?

2ND MACBETH.
> Who was the Thane lives yet, but under heavy judgement
> Bears that life which he deserves to lose
> But treasons capital, confessed and proved
> Have overthrown him.

MACBETH.
> Do you not hope that your children shall be kings
> When those that gave the Thane of Cawdor to me
> Promised no less to them?

BANQUO.
> That trusted home
> Might yet enkindle you unto the crown
> Besides the Thane of Cawdor. But tis strange.

(MACBETH gives BANQUO one last look and strides out. MACBETHS 1 and 2 superciliously confront a startled BANQUO. The group stands motionless until LADY MACBETH strides between them commencing the next scene, and then they vanish)

LADY MACBETH.
> Glamis thou art, and Cawdor, and shalt be
> What thou art promised.

1ST WITCH.
> The King comes here tonight.

LADY MACBETH.
> Thou'rt mad to say it!

1ST WITCH.
> So please you, it is true. Our Thane is coming;

LADY MACBETH.
> The raven himself is hoarse
> That croaks the fatal entrance of Duncan
> Under my battlements.

(During this speech, WITCHES come forward and take
hold of LADY MACBETH. They whisper the words
she speaks)

(formally, as invocation)
Come, you spirits
That tend on mortal thoughts, unsex me here
And fill me from the crown to the toe top-full
Of direst cruelty. Make thick my blood;
Stop up the access and passage to remorse,
That no compunctious visitings of nature
Shake my fell purpose, nor keep peace between
The effect and it. Come to my woman's breasts
And take my milk for gall, you murdering ministers,
Wherever, in your sightless substances,
You wait on nature's mischief. Come, thick night,
And pall thee in the dunnest smoke of hell,
That my keen knife see not the wound it makes,
Nor heaven peep through the blanket of the dark
To cry, 'Hold, hold!'

(WITCHES take up position behind LADY MACBETH,
facing upstage. Enter MACBETH)

Great Glamis, worthy Cawdor!
Greater than both by the all-hail hereafter!
Thy letters have transported me beyond
This ignorant present and I feel now
The future in the instant.

MACBETH.
    My dearest love. (They kiss)
    Duncan comes here tonight.

LADY MACBETH.
    And when goes hence?

MACBETH.
    Tomorrow, as he purposes.

LADY MACBETH.
    O never
    Shall sun that morrow see!

(Cut to:)

DUNCAN.
    O worthiest cousin!
    The sin of my ingratitude even now
    Was heavy on me. Thou art so far before,
    That swiftest wing of recompense is slow
    To overtake thee. Would thou hadst less deserved,
    That the proportion both of thanks and payment
    Might have been mine. Only I have left to say,
    'More is thy due than more than all can pay.'

MACBETH.
    The service and the loyalty I owe,
    In doing it, pays itself. Your highness' part
    Is to receive our duties; and our duties
    Are to your throne and state, children and servants,
    Which do but what they should by doing everything
    Safe toward your love and honour.

KING.
    I have begun to plant thee, and will labour
    To make thee full of growing.

LADY MACBETH.
    Your face, my thane, is as a book where men
    May read strange matters. To beguile the time
    Look like the time, bear welcome in your eye,
    Your hand, your tongue: He that's coming
    Must be provided for.

BANQUO.
    I dreamt last night of the three weird sisters.
    To you they have showed some truth.

MACBETH.
    I think not of them.

LADY MACBETH.
    I will acquaint you with the perfect spy o' the time
    The moment on't; for it must be done tonight.

MACBETH.
    We will speak further.

BANQUO.
    Yet, when we can entreat an hour to serve,
    We would spend it in some words upon that business
    If you grant the time.

LADY MACBETH.
    Put this night's great business into my dispatch.
    It shall make honour for you.

MACBETH. (to LADY MACBETH harshly)
    So I lose none
    In seeking to augment it, but still keep
    My bosom franchis'd and allegiance clear.

BANQUO.
    Good repose the while.

MACBETH.
    Thanks sir, the like to you.

LADY MACBETH.
    Leave all the rest to me.

MACBETH.
    We - will - speak - further.

(LADY MACBETH and BANQUO, speaking simultaneously, repeat the words of their scene. Pouring them, like liquid, into MACBETH's ears)

BANQUO.	LADY MACBETH.
I dreamt last night of the three weird sisters.	I will acquaint you with the perfect spy o' the time
To you they have showed some truth	The moment of it for it must be done tonight
Yet when we can entreat an hour	Put this night's great business into my dispatch
We would spend it in some words upon that business	It shall make honour for you. Leave all the rest to me.

If you grant the time.
Good repose the while.

(As MACBETH cuts downstage, he is confronted by
MACBETHS 2 and 3. BANQUO and LADY MACBETH
exit)

MACBETH. (reasoning)
He's here in double trust:
First, as I am his kinsman and his subject,
Strong both against the deed; then, as his host,
Who should against his murderer shut the door,
Not bear the knife myself.

2ND MACBETH. (facetious)
Besides, this Duncan
Hath borne his faculties so meek, hath been
So clear in his great office, that his virtues
Will plead like angels, trumpet-tongued against
The deep damnation of his taking-off;

3RD MACBETH.
And Pity, like a naked new-born babe
Striding the blast, or heaven's cherubim, horsed
Upon the sightless couriers of the air,
Shall blow the horrid deed in every eye,
That tears shall drown the wind.

(Pause. MACBETHS 2 and 3 regard the petrified
MACBETH)

2ND MACBETH. (to MACBETH 3)
Were I king,
I should cut off the Nobles for their lands,
Desire his jewels, and this other's house,
And my more-having would be as a sauce
To make me hunger more.

3RD MACBETH. (to 2ND MACBETH)
Were I king,
Your wives, your daughters
Your matrons and your maids could not fill up
The cistern of my lust.

2ND MACBETH.
>I should forge
>Quarrels unjust against the good and loyal,
>Destroying them for their wealth.

3RD MACBETH.
>I should
>Pour the sweet milk of concord into Hell
>Uproar the universal peace, confound
>All unity on earth.

MACBETH. (trying to blot out the thoughts of MACBETHS 2 and 3)
>Stars, hide your fires,
>Let not light see my black and deep desires,
>The eye wink at the hand; yet let that be
>Which the eye fears, when it is done, to see.

3RD MACBETH.
>Thou wouldst be great
>Art not without ambition, but without
>The illness should attend it.
>Wouldst not play false.

2ND MACBETH.
>And yet would wrongly win.
>Thou'dst have great Glamis
>That which cries 'Thus thou must do' if thou have it,
>And that which rather thou does fear to do
>Than wishest should be undone.

MACBETH.
>I have no spur
>To prick the sides of my intent but only...

2ND MACBETH. (snide)
>Vaulting ambition which o'erleaps itself
>And falls on the other.

3RD MACBETH. (exhorting)
>Was the hope drunk
>Wherein you dressed yourself?

2ND MACBETH.
>Art thou afear'd to be the same in thine act and
> valour as thou art in desire?
>When you durst do it, then you were a man.

MACBETH. (lamely rationalizing)
>My thought, whose murder yet is but fantastical,
>Shakes so my single state of man
>That function is smothered in surmise.

2ND MACBETH. (washing hands of him)
>Go prick thy face and over-red thy fear,
>Thou lily-livered boy!

3RD MACBETH. (reasoning)
>Present fears are less than horrible imaginings.

2ND MACBETH. (still ill-temper'd)
>Blood hath been shed ere now.

(MACBETH hesitates. MACBETHS 2 and 3 close in)

3RD MACBETH.
>Laugh to scorn
>The power of man.

2ND MACBETH.
>For none of woman-born
>Shall harm Macbeth.

(Daggers are placed into his grip)

MACBETH (quietly)
>Thou marshall'st me the way I was going
>And such an instrument I was to use...

3RD MACBETH.
>Come what come may,
>Time and the hour runs through the roughest day.

(MACBETHS 1 and 2 arrange his stance so that it
suggests a murderer about to strike. Then step back)

MACBETH. (with daggers)
>   I am settled; and bend up
>   Each corporal agent to this terrible feat.
>   From this moment,
>   The very firstlings of my heart shall be
>   The firstlings of my hand.

2ND MACBETH. (gaily)
>   Away

3RD MACBETH.
>   And mock the time

2ND MACBETH.
>   with fairest show,

3RD MACBETH.
>   False face

2ND MACBETH.
>   must hide

3RD MACBETH.
>   what the false heart

2ND MACBETH.
>   doth know.

>   (A sepulchral bell begins to toll in the distance.
>   LADY MACBETH and WITCHES congregate around
>   MACBETH who stands transfixed with daggers)

MACBETH.
>   Now o'er the one half-world
>   Nature seems dead, and wicked dreams abuse
>   The curtained sleep. Witchcraft celebrates
>   Pale Hecate's offerings; and withered murder,
>   Alarumed by his sentinel the wolf,
>   Whose howl's his watch, thus with his stealthy pace,
>   With Tarquin's ravishing strides, towards his design
>   Moves like a ghost. Thou sure and firm-set earth,
>   Hear not my steps, which way they walk, for fear
>   The very stones prate of my whereabout

And take the present horror from the time
Which now suits with it. Whilst I threat, he lives:
Words to the heat of deeds too cold breath gives.

(Tolling continues)

I go, and it is done; the bell invites me.
Hear it not, Duncan, for it is a knell
That summons thee to heaven or to hell.

(Exit)

(Lights fade up dimly on Duncan's chamber. MACBETHS 1 and 2 play Duncan's grooms) (GROOMS are discovered dicing at foot of Duncan's bed. WITCHES arrive, lure the GROOMS to drink. When GROOMS topple over drunk, WITCHES circle DUNCAN's bed and take up formal positions. During this opening action, the VOICE of LADY MACBETH has been heard (on tape) speaking the accompanying speech)

VOICE OF LADY MACBETH.
When Duncan is asleep,
Whereto the rather shall
  his day's hard journey
  Soundly invite him - his
  two chamberlains
Will I with wine and
  wassail so convince
That memory, the
  warder of the brain,
Shall be a'fume, and the
  receipt of reason
a Limbeck only. When
  in swinish sleep
Their drenched natures
  lie as in a death,
What cannot you and I
  perform upon
The unguarded Duncan?
  What not put upon
His spongy officers, who
  shall bear the guilt
Of our great quell.

(When the WITCHES are in position around the bed, they begin chanting a prayer for the dead, the text of which is alongside. The speech is on tape as well as whispered during

Witches' Prayer
One cried 'God bless us'
  and 'Amen' the other
As they had seen me with
  these hangman's hands.
Listening their fear I
  could not say 'Amen'

the scene)

(MACBETH, with bloody hands, slowly enters the chamber. He stands hesitating for a moment, then proceeds towards the bed. The drunk GROOMS stir. He stops. Waits. Then moves forward again. One of the GROOMS, having a nightmare, suddenly shakes himself awake with a cry which rouses the other. Both now awake, confront MAC- BETH and stare at his hands. Then, strangely calm, in no way surprised by MACBETH's presence in the chamber, they kneel and begin to pray. MAC- BETH watches them for a moment, and then blesses them. With each blessing a GROOM topples over dead until both are lying motionless on the floor. The WITCHES place two daggers into MACBETH's hands, and, still praying, usher him over to the sleeping DUNCAN. The WITCHES then hoist up the sleeping KING and present him to MACBETH. DUN- CAN, now roused from sleep, confronts MAC- BETH, his eyes wild and frightened. MACBETH raises the daggers and then lowers them. Con- tinues staring into

When they did say 'God bless us'.
But wherefore could not I pronounce 'Amen'?
I had most need of blessing, and 'Amen' Stuck in my throat.
Methought I heard a voice cry 'Sleep no more'
Macbeth does murder sleep - the innocent sleep
Sleep that knits up the ravelled sleeve of care,
The death of each day's life, sore labour's bath,
Balm of hurt minds, great nature's second course,
Chief nourisher in life's feast.
Still it cried 'Sleep no more' to all the house;
'Glamis hath murder'd sleep, and therefore Cawdor
Shall sleep no more, Macbeth shall sleep no more'.

> DUNCAN's terrified eyes..
> Raises his daggers again.
> At that moment, LADY
> MACBETH appears, takes
> hold of MACBETH's hands
> and drives the daggers
> into DUNCAN's heart.
> There is an ear-splitting
> cry from DUNCAN which
> is picked up by the
> WITCHES. All vanish
> immediately on the
> Blackout.

(Lights up. MACDUFF enters)

MACDUFF.
    O horror, horror, horror!
    Tongue nor heart cannot conceive nor name thee'.
    Confusion now hath made his masterpiece;
    Most sacrilegious murder hath broke ope
    The Lord's anointed temple and stole thence
    The life o' the building.
    Awake, awake!
    Ring the alarum bell! Murder and treason!
    Banquo and Donalbain, Malcolm, awake!
    Shake off this downy sleep, death's counterfeit,
    And look on death itself! Up, up, and see
    The Great Doom's image! Malcolm, Banquo,
    As from your graves rise up and walk like sprites
    To countenance this horror. Ring the bell!

(Bell rings. Real bell now sounds. Enter LADY MACBETH. During scene, WITCHES stand motionless in background)

LADY MACBETH.
    What's the business,
    That such a hideous trumpet calls to parley
    The sleepers of the house? Speak, speak!

MACDUFF.
    O gentle lady,

'Tis not for you to hear what I can speak.
The repetition in a woman's ear
Would murder as it fell.

(Enter BANQUO)

O Banquo, Banquo!
Our royal master's murdered.

LADY MACBETH.
Woe, alas!
What, in our house!

BANQUO.
Too cruel, anywhere.
Dear Duff, I prithee contradict thyself
And say it is not so.

(Enter MACBETHS)

2ND MACBETH.
Had I but died an hour before this chance
I had lived a blessed time.

(Enter MALCOLM)

MALCOLM.
What is amiss?

3RD MACBETH.
You are, and do not know't.
The spring, the head, the fountain of your blood
Is stopped, the very source of it is stopped.

MACDUFF.
Your royal father's murdered.

MALCOLM.
By whom?

2ND MACBETH.
Those of his chamber, as it seemed, had done't:
Their hands and faces were all badged with blood,

So were their daggers, which, unwiped, we found
Upon their pillows; they stared and were distracted;
No man's life was to be trusted with them.

MACBETH.
O yet I do repent me of my fury,
That I did kill them.

MACDUFF.
Wherefore did you so?

MACBETH.
Who can be wise, amazed, temperate and furious,
Loyal and neutral, in a moment? No man. (knocking)
The expedition of my violent love
Outruns the pauser reason. (knocking) Here lay Duncan,
His silver skin laced with his golden blood,
And his gashed stabs looked like a breach in nature
For ruin's wasteful entrance, (knocking) there the murderers
Steeped in colours of their trade, their daggers (knocking)
unmannerly breeched with gore. Who could refrain,
That had a heart to love, and in that heart
Courage to make's love known?

(For a moment no-one speaks. All regard MACBETH's hands. He then looks down at them as well)

LADY MACBETH. (swooning)
Help me hence, ho!

MACDUFF.
Look to the lady!

BANQUO. (to MACDUFF)
Why do we hold our tongues,
That most may claim this argument for ours?

MALCOLM.
What should be spoken here where our fate,
Hid in an auger-hole, may rush and seize us?
Let's away. Our tears are not yet brewed.

MACDUFF.
    Nor our strong sorrow upon the foot of motion.

BANQUO.
    And when we have our naked frailties hid
    That suffer in exposure, let us meet
    And question this most bloody piece of work
    Fears and scruples shake us.
    In the great hand of God I stand, and thence,
    Against the indivulg'd pretence, I fight
    Of treasonous malice.

MACDUFF.
    And so do I.

MALCOLM.
    And so do I.

BANQUO.
    And so do all. (They pledge and exit)

    (Sepulchral knocking is heard by MACBETH)

MACBETH.
    Whence is that knocking?
    How is't with me when every noise appalls me?
    What hands are here! Ha - they pluck out mine eyes!

    (WITCHES with MACBETH effigy during speech)

    Will all great Neptune's ocean wash this blood
    Clean from my hand? No, this my hand will rather
    The multitudinous seas incarnadine,
    Making the green one red.

    (Enter LADY MACBETH. Sepulchral knocking
    becomes real)

2ND MACBETH. I hear a knocking at the south entry.
3RD MACBETH. Retire we to our chamber.
                A little water clears us of this deed.
2ND MACBETH. Your constancy hath left you unattended.
3RD MACBETH. Hark! More knocking!

2ND MACBETH. Get on your nightgown, lest occasion
                                          (call us
                    And show us to be watchers.
                    Be not lost so poorly in your thoughts.

   (They exit)

MACBETH.
     To know my deed 'twere best not know myself.

     (Knocking persists. MACBETH approaches door,
     opens it, a bloody DUNCAN - in shroud - appears on
     threshold. Blackout. On DUNCAN's appearance, the
     WITCHES emit a fearful but exaggerated cry of
     fright and, on Blackout, come downstage - sans
     stocking masks)

2ND WITCH. (of DUNCAN)
     What bloody man is that?

     (All laugh)

3RD WITCH.
     Who would have thought the old man had so much blood
     in him.

     (All laugh)

3RD WITCH. (parodying MACBETH)
     I have done the deed.

     (2ND WITCH blows raspberry)

3RD WITCH.
     Dids't thou hear a noise?

1ST WITCH.
     I hear the owl scream and the cricket cry.

66

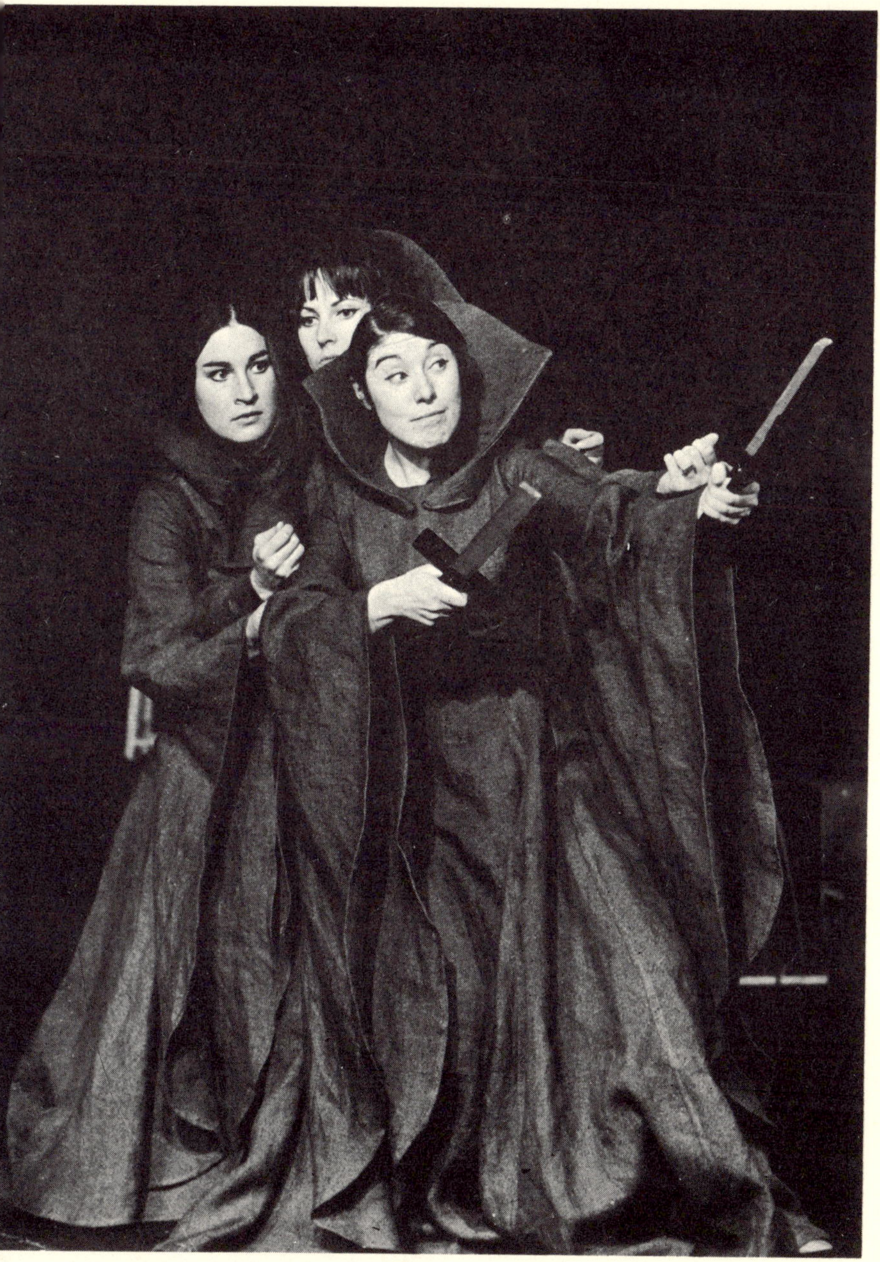

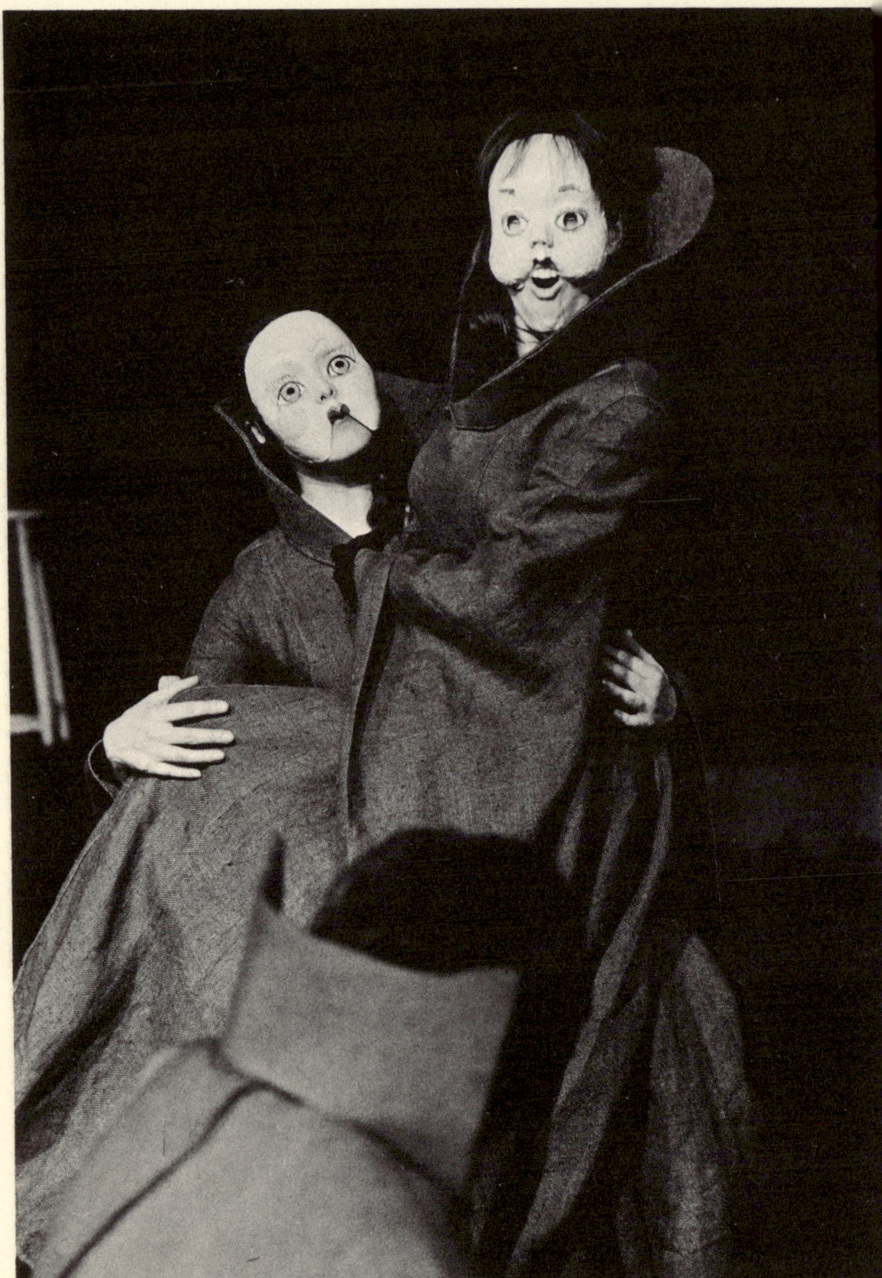

Did not you speak?

2ND WITCH.
    When?

1ST WITCH.
    Now.

2ND WITCH.
    As I descended?

1ST WITCH.
    Ay. (Giggles)

    (All laugh together)

2ND WITCH.
    Who lies in the second chamber?

3RD WITCH.
    Donalbain.

2ND WITCH. (peering into 3RD WITCH's face)
    This is a sorry sight.

1ST WITCH. (irritated)
    A foolish thought to say a sorry sight.
    (peers into 3RD WITCH's face)
    This is a sorry sight.
    Why did you bring these daggers from the place?
    They must lie there. Go, carry them and smear
    The sleepy grooms with blood.

2ND WITCH. (banging the ground mock-tragically)
    I'll go no more.
    I am afraid to think what I have done;
    Look on't again I dare not.

1ST WITCH.
    Infirm of purpose! Give me the bloody daggers.
    (She takes them melodramatically, then focuses as if
    seeing them for the first time)
    Is this a dagger I see before me

69

The handle toward my hand?
Come let me clutch thee.
I have thee not. Yet I see thee still.
Art thou not, fatal vision, sensible to feeling as to sight?
Or art thou but a dagger of the mind; a false creation
Proceeding from the heat-oppress'd brain.

(WITCHES applaud 1ST WITCH's performance. 1ST WITCH takes a bow. Then suddenly takes up purposeful stance)

I go and it is done; the bell invites me.

WITCHES. (piping high)
Ting-a-ling-a-ling.

1ST WITCH.
Hear it not Duncan, for it is a knell.

WITCHES. (high)
Ting-a-ling-a-ling.

1ST WITCH.
That summons thee to heaven.

WITCHES. (high)
Ting-a-ling-a-ling.

1ST WITCH.
Or to hell.

WITCHES. (in bass register)
Ting-a-ling-a-ling.

(WITCHES begin to stalk out, all moving forward with the same foot. 1ST WITCH suddenly notices MACBETH, shushes them, they regain their composure, pull on their masks and quickly depart. MACBETH is rolled downstage in an oversize throne pushed by MACBETHS 1 and 2. His feet dangle without touching the floor. He looks like a baby in a high-chair)

MACBETH.
    To be thus...

2ND MACBETH.
    is nothing!

3RD MACBETH.
    But to be safely thus!

2ND MACBETH.
    Our fears in Banquo
    Stick deep; and in his royalty of nature
    Reigns that which would be feared.

3RD MACBETH.
    Tis much he dares,
    And to that dauntless temper of his mind
    He hath a wisdom that doth guide his valour
    To act in safety.

2ND MACBETH.
    He chid the sisters
    When first they put the name of king upon thee
    And bade them speak to him.

3RD MACBETH.
    Then prophet-like,
    They hailed him father to a line of kings.

2ND MACBETH.
    Upon thy head they placed a fruitless crown
    And put a barren sceptre in thy grip
    Thence to be wrenched with an unlineal hand
    No son of thine succeeding.

MACBETH.
    If it be so
    For Banquo's issue have I filed my mind,
    For them the gracious Duncan have I murdered,
    Put rancours in the vessel of my peace,
    Only for them; and mine eternal jewel
    Given to the common enemy of man.

2ND MACBETH.
    To make them kings.

3RD MACBETH.
    The seed of Banquo, kings.

MACBETH.
    Rather than so, come fate into the list
    And champion me to the utterance.

    (BANQUO enters)

    Here's our chief guest.
    If he had been forgot
    It had been as a gap in our great feast
    And all-thing unbecoming.

    (All freeze during BANQUO's next speech)

BANQUO.
    Thou hast it now: King, Cawdor, Glamis, all
    As the weird woman promised; and I fear
    Thou playd'st most foully for't. Yet it was said
    It should not stand in thy posterity
    But that myself should be the root and father
    of many kings. If there come truth from them
    As upon thee, Macbeth, their speeches shine,
    Why by the verities on thee made good
    May they not be my oracles as well
    And set me up in hope?

    (Motion)

MACBETH.
    Tonight we hold a solemn supper, sir
    And I'll request your presence.

BANQUO.
    Let your highness
    Command upon me, to the which my duties
    Are with a most indissoluble tie
    Forever knit.

MACBETH.
> Ride you this afternoon?

BANQUO.
> Ay, my good lord.

(Static)

2ND MACBETH.
> I am one, my liege,
> Whom the vile blows and buffets of the world,
> Hath so incens'd that I am reckless what I do
> To spite the world.

MACBETH.
> Is it far you ride?

3RD MACBETH.
> And I another,
> So weary with disasters, tugged with fortune,
> That I would set my life on any chance
> To mend it or be rid on't.

(Motion)

BANQUO.
> As far my lord, as will fill up the time
> Twixt this and supper. Go not my horse the better,
> I must become a borrower of the night
> For a dark hour or twain.

MACBETH.
> Fail not our feast.

BANQUO.
> My lord, I will not.

(Static)

MACBETH.
> Every minute of his being thrusts against
> My near'st of life. It must be done tonight.

2ND MACBETH.
    It is concluded!

3RD MACBETH.
    Banquo, thy soul's flight,
    If it find heaven, must find it out tonight.

(Motion)

MACBETH.
    Hie you to horse. Adieu.
    Till you return tonight. Goes Fleance with you?

BANQUO.
    Ay my good lord; (pause) our time does call upon's.

MACBETH.
    I wish your horses swift and sure of foot
    And so I do commend you to their backs.
    Farewell.
    Let every man be master of his time
    Till seven at night. Farewell.

(BANQUO exits, Murderers - MACBETHS 1 and 2 -
follow on each side. Simultaneously, double-bed is
rolled down. LADY MACBETH under sheet;
WITCHES beside her)

LADY MACBETH.
    Is Banquo gone from court?

WITCH.
    Ay madam, but returns again tonight.

LADY MACBETH. (secretly content)
    Say to the King I would attend his leisure
    For a few words...

(Settles back in bed. The WITCHES have not moved;
each is silently communing with the other.
Eventually, LADY MACBETH becomes aware of the
hesitation; turns to 1ST WITCH)

WITCH. (caught)
>Madam, I will.

>(WITCHES in background, stand awaiting LADY MACBETH's instructions)

LADY MACBETH. (as MACBETH enters)
>How now, my Lord? Why do you keep alone,
>Of sorriest fancies your companions making,
>Using those thoughts which should indeed have died
>With them they think on? Things without all remedy
>Should be without regard; what's done is done.

MACBETH.
>What is the night?

LADY MACBETH.
>Almost at odds with morning which is which.
>Come, we'll to sleep.

>(WITCHES begin whispering into MACBETH's ears)

MACBETH.
>We have scorched the snake, not killed it;
>She'll close and be herself, whilst our poor malice
>Remains in danger of her former tooth.
>But let the frame of things disjoint, both the worlds suffer
>Ere we will eat our meal in fear, and sleep
>In the affliction of these terrible dreams
>That shake us nightly; better be with the dead
>Whom we, to gain our peace, have sent to peace,
>Than on the torture of the mind to lie
>In restless ecstasy. Duncan is in his grave;
>After life's fitful fever he sleeps well;
>Treason has done his worst. Nor steel, nor poison,
>Malice domestic, foreign levy, nothing
>Can touch him further.

LADY MACBETH.
>Come on,
>Gentle my lord, sleek o'er your rugged looks,
>Be bright and novial among your guests tonight.

MACBETH.
>O, full of scorpions is my mind, dear wife.

(WITCHES abruptly stop whispering. LADY MACBETH consolingly embraces MACBETH)

>There's comfort yet!
>Ere the bat hath flown
>His cloistered flight, ere to black Hecate's summons
>The shard-borne beetle, with his drowsy hums,
>Hath run night's yawning peal, there shall be done
>A deed of dreadful note.

LADY MACBETH.
>What's to be done?

MACBETH.
>Be innocent of the knowledge, dearest chuck,
>Till thou applaud the deed.

(MACBETH exits. WITCHES congregate around LADY MACBETH and take up formal positions. During following invocation, WITCHES whisper LADY MACBETH's words)

LADY MACBETH.
>Come, seeling night
>Scarf up the tender eye of pitiful day,
>And with thy bloody and invisible hand
>Cancel and tear to pieces that great bond
>Which keeps me pale. Light thickens
>And the crow makes wing to the rooky wood;
>Good things of day begin to droop and drowse
>While night's black agents to their preys do rouse.

(The two MACBETHS suddenly appear illuminated. They beckon to MACBETH who joins them)

2ND MACBETH.
>Come stand with us;

The west yet glimmers with some streaks of day.
Now spurs the lated traveller apace
To gain the timely inn; and near approaches
The subject of our watch.

3RD MACBETH.
Hark, I hear horses!

BANQUO. (within)
Give us a light there, ho!

2ND MACBETH.
Then 'tis he.
The rest that are within the note of expectation,
Already are i' the court.

3RD MACBETH.
His horses go about.

2ND MACBETH.
Almost a mile; but he does usually.
So all men do, from hence to the palace gate
Make it their walk.

(Enter BANQUO and FLEANCE, with a torch)

3RD MACBETH.
A light, a light!

2ND MACBETH.
'Tis he.

3RD MACBETH.
Stand to 't!

BANQUO.
It will be rain tonight.

1ST MACBETH.
Let it come down!

BANQUO.
Fly Good Fleance. Fly. Fly. Fly.

(They attack BANQUO. A net is dropped onto BANQUO who is suddenly hoisted up and swung in space. While MACBETHS stab their prey in the trap, WITCHES, at side, tear strips off BANQUO's effigy revealing bright red colouring underneath. Simultaneously, banquet table is brought out and guests, led by MACBETH, enter in a dance around table. All assemble for banquet, chatting and laughing. But when seated, only WITCHES and MACBETH are at table. The dance ends drunkenly and breathless)

MACBETH.
You know your own degrees, sit down. At first
And last, the hearty welcome.
Ourself will mingle with society
And play the humble host.
Our hostess keeps her state; but in best time
We will require her welcome.

LADY MACBETH.
Pronounce it for me, sir, to all our friends,
For my heart speaks they are welcome.

MACBETH.
See, they encounter thee with their hearts' thanks;
Both sides are even
Be large in mirth. Anon we'll drink a measure
The table round.

LADY MACBETH. (aside)
There's blood upon thy face.

MACBETH. (aside)
'Tis Banquo's then,
Safe in a ditch he bides
With twenty trenched gashes in his head
The least a death to nature.
LADY MACBETH.
My royal lord,
You do not give the cheer. The feast is sold
That is not often vouched, while 'tis a-making,
'Tis given with welcome. To feed were best at home;
From thence, the sauce to meat is ceremony;

Meeting were bare without it.

MACBETH.
Sweet remembrancer!
Now good digestion wait on appetite,
And health on both!

ALL.
Health on both!

(Enter the GHOST OF BANQUO and sits in
MACBETH's place. All at table become strangely still,
smiling knowingly at each other)

MACBETH.
Here had we now our country's honour roofed,
Were the graced person of our Banquo present;
Who may I rather challenge for unkindness
Than pity for mischance.

3RD MACBETH (with knowing smile)
His absence, sir,
Lays blame upon his promise. Pleas't your highness
To grace us with your royal company?

MACBETH.
The table's full.

2ND MACBETH (sharing the joke)
Here is a place reserved, sir.

MACBETH.
Where?

2ND MACBETH.
Here, my good lord. What is't that moves your
highness?

MACBETH.
Which of you have done this?

ALL.
What, my good lord?

MACBETH.
>Thou canst not say I did it; never shake
>Thy gory locks at me.

3RD MACBETH. (smiling, unperturbed, remaining seated)
>Gentlemen, rise. His highness is not well.

LADY MACBETH.
>Sit, worthy friends. My Lord is often thus;
>The fit is momentary; upon a thought
>He will again be well.

MACBETH.
>Behold! (All at table become animate again; talking laughing, etc.)

LADY MACBETH.
>O proper stuff!
>This is the very painting of your fear.
>This is the air-drawn dagger which you said
>Led you to Duncan. O, these flaws and starts,
>Imposters to true fear, would well become
>A woman's story at a winter's fire,
>Authorized by her grandam. Shame itself!
>Why do you make such faces? When all's done
>You look but on a stool.

MACBETH.
>Look! Lo! - How say you? (All freeze as before)
>Why, what care I if thou canst nod! Speak, too!
>If charnel-houses and our graves must send
>Those that we bury back, our monuments
>Shall be the maws of kites.

3RD MACBETH.
>Quite unmanned in folly?

LADY MACBETH.
>Fie, for shame!

MACBETH.
>The times has been
>That, when the brains were out, the man would die,

And there an end. But now they rise again
With twenty mortal murders on their crowns,
And push us from our stools.

LADY MACBETH.
    My worthy lord,
    Your noble friends do lack you.

(The table becomes animate again)

MACBETH. (attempts to ignore the GHOST)
    I do forget.
    Do not muse at me, my most worthy friends:
    I have a strange infirmity, which is nothing
    To those that know me. Come, love and health to
      all!
    Then I'll sit down. Give me some wine; fill full!

(BANQUO empties his blood into goblet and proffers
it to MACBETH. All freeze into tableau)

Avaunt, and quit my sight! Let the earth hide thee!
Thy bones are marrowless, thy blood is cold.
Thou hast no speculation in those eyes
Which thou dost glare with.
What man dare, I dare.
Approach thou like the rugged Russian bear,
The armed rhinoceros, or the Hyrcan tiger,
Take any shape but that, and my firm nerves
Shall never tremble. Or be alive again,
And dare me to the desert with thy sword:
If trembling I inhabit then, protest me
The baby of a girl. Hence, horrible shadow!
Unreal mockery, hence!

(Upsets table. Pandemonium. All exit)

(Cut into new scene)

MACBETH.
    I conjure you, by that which you profess,
    Howe'er you come to know it, answer me -
    Though you untie the winds and let them fight
    Against the churches; though the yesty waves
    Confound and swallow navigation up;
    Though bladed corn be lodged and trees blown down;
    Though castles topple on their warders' heads;
    Though palaces and pyramids do slope
    Their heads to their foundations: though the treasure
    Of nature's germens tumble all together
    Even till destruction sicken - answer me
    To what I ask you.

1ST WITCH.
    Speak.

2ND WITCH.
    Demand.

3RD WITCH.
    We'll answer.

1ST WITCH.
    Say if thou'dst rather hear it from our mouths
    Or from our masters.

MACBETH.
    Call 'em. Let me see 'em.

ALL.
    Come high or low,
    Thyself and office deftly show.

    (Thunder. 1ST APPARITION. Dead DUNCAN IS
    raised up. Eyes cavernous-black. WITCHES hold
    him up to speak through him. MACBETH starts but
    3RD WITCH calms him)

MACBETH.
    Tell me, thou unknown power -

1ST WITCH.
>He knows thy thought.
>Hear his speech, say thou naught.

1ST APPARITION. (Spoken by 1ST WITCH)
>Macbeth, Macbeth, Macbeth, beware Macduff!
>Beware the Thane of Fife! Dismiss me. Enough.

>(He descends into trap)

MACBETH.
>Whate'er thou art, for thy good caution, thanks;
>Thou hast harped my fear aright. But one word more -

1ST WITCH.
>He will not be commanded. Here's another
>More potent than the first.

>(Thunder.   2ND APPARITION.   Dead BANQUO
>raised up)

2ND APPARITION.
>Macbeth, Macbeth, Macbeth!

MACBETH.
>Had I three ears, I'd hear thee.

2ND APPARITION. (Spoken by 2ND WITCH)
>Be bloody, bold, and resolute; laugh to scorn
>The power of man; for none of woman born
>Shall harm Macbeth.

>(He descends)

MACBETH.
>Then live Macduff; what need I fear of theee?
>But yet I'll make assurance double sure,
>And take a bond of fate. Thou shalt not live;
>That I may tell pale-hearted fear it lies,
>And sleep in spite of thunder.

>(Thunder.   3RD APPARITION.   2ND MACBETH
>wearing mask of MACBETH)

1ST WITCH.
    Listen, but speak not to 't.

3RD APPARITION. (Spoken by 3RD WITCH)
    Be lion-mettled, proud, and take no care
    Who chafes, who frets, or where conspirers are;
    Macbeth shall never vanquished be, until
    Great Birnam Wood to high Dunsinane Hill
    Shall come against him.

MACBETH.
    That will never be.
    Who can impress the forest, bid the tree
    Unfix his earth-bound root? Sweet bodements! Good!
    Rebellious dead rise never till the wood
    Of Birnam rise, and our high-placed Macbeth
    Shall live the lease of nature, pay his breath
    To time and mortal custom. Yet my heart
    Throbs to know one thing: tell me, if your art
    Can tell so much, shall Banquo's issue ever
    Reign in this kingdom?

ALL.
    Seek to know no more.

    (2ND MACBETH descends)

MACBETH.
    I will be satisfied! Deny me this
    And an eternal curse fall on you!

    (WITCH-chord)

    And what noise is this?

1ST WITCH.
    Show!

2ND WITCH.
    Show!

3RD WITCH.
    Show!

ALL.
    Show his eyes and grieve his heart;
    Come like shadows, so depart.

    (WITCHES in a queue behind MACBETH take turns
    putting hands over his eyes)

MACBETH.
    Thou art too like the spirit of Banquo. Down!
    Thy crown does sear mine eye-balls.

NEXT WITCH.
    Thou other gold-bound brow, is like the first.

NEXT WITCH.
    A third is like the former. - Filthy hags,
    Why do you show me this?

NEXT WITCH.
    A fourth? Start, eyes!
    What, will the line stretch out to the crack of doom?

NEXT WITCH.
    Another yet?

NEXT WITCH.
    A seventh? I'll see no more!

NEXT WITCH.
    And yet the eighth appears, who bears a glass
    Which shows me many more. And some I see
    That two-fold balls and treble sceptres carry.

    (Dead BANQUO with crown is now thrust before
    MACBETH)

Horrible sight! Now I see 'tis true,
For the blood-boltered Banquo smiles upon me,
And points at them for his. What! Is this so?

1ST WITCH.
Ay, sir, all this is so.

2ND WITCH. (tracing a vision)
Hark, I did hear the galloping of horses.

3RD WITCH. (divining the vision from 2ND WITCH)
Macduff is fled to England.

(All turn to MACBETH, as if to say: 'What will you do now?')

MACBETH.
From this moment
The very firstlings of my heart shall be
The firstlings of my hand.
The castle of Macduff I will surprise,
Seize upon Fife, give to the end o' the sword
His wife, his babes, and all unfortunate souls
That trace him in his line, and even now,
To crown my thoughts with acts, be it thought and
 done.
Come you secret black and midnight hags,
Bring me where they are.

(WITCHES, taking masks, assume characters of LADY MACDUFF and CHILD. LADY MACDUFF takes babe in her arms. Scene is played out like an old-fashioned Morality play - in a crude, artificial style)

WIFE.
Sirrah, your father's dead.
And what will you do now? How will you live?

SON.
As birds do, mother.

WIFE.
What, with worms and flies?

SON.
> With what I get, I mean; and so do they.
> My father is not dead, for all your saying.

WIFE.
> Yes, he is dead. How wilt thou do for a father?

SON.
> Nay, how will you do for a husband?

WIFE.
> Why, I can buy me twenty at any market.

SON.
> Then you'll buy 'em to sell again.

WIFE.
> Thou speak'st with all thy wit;
> And yet, i' faith, with wit enough for thee.

SON.
> Was my father a traitor, mother?

WIFE.
> Ay, that he was.

SON.
> What is a traitor?

WIFE.
> Why, one that swears and lies.

SON.
> And be all traitors that do so?

WIFE.
> Every one that does so is a traitor,
> And must be hanged.

SON.
> And must they all be hanged that swear and lie?

WIFE.
>   Every one.

SON.
>   Who must hang them?

WIFE.
>   Why, the honest men.

SON.
>   Then the liars and swearers are fools; for there are
>   liars and swearers enow to beat the honest men and
>   hang
>   up them.

WIFE.
>   Now God help thee, poor monkey!   But how wilt
>   thou do for a father?

SON.
>   If he were dead, you'd weep for him; if you would
>   not, it were a good sign that I should quickly have
>   a new father.

WIFE.
>   Poor prattler, how thou talk'st!

>   (3RD WITCH as male is cued on by 1ST WITCH -
>   irritably because cue was missed)

>   Poor prattler, how thou talk'st!

3RD WITCH.
>   Bless you, fair dame! I am not to you known,
>   Though in your state of honour I am perfect.
>   I doubt some danger does approach you nearly.
>   If you will take a homely man's advice,
>   Be not found here. Hence with your little ones!
>   To fright you thus methinks I am too savage;
>   To do worse to you were fell cruelty,
>   Which is too nigh your person. Heaven preserve you!
>   I dare abide no longer.
>   (Exit)

WIFE.
>   Whither should I fly?
>   I have done no harm. But I remember now
>   I am in this earthly world, where to do harm
>   Is often laudable, to do good sometime
>   Accounted dangerous folly. Why then, alas,
>   Do I put up that womanly defence
>   To say I have done no harm?

(Enter murderers - MACBETHS 2 and 3)

WIFE.
>   What are these faces?

2ND MACBETH.
>   Where is your husband?

WIFE.
>   I hope in no place so unsanctified
>   Where such as thou mayst find him.

3RD MACBETH.
>   He's a traitor.

SON.
>   Thou liest, thou shag-haired villain!

3RD MACBETH.
>   What, you egg,
>   Young fry of treachery!

(LADY MACDUFF and BABE are stalked then cornered. Then, daggers are thrust into MACBETH's hands and he is forced to stab LADY MACDUFF and SON. As dagger enters SON, MACDUFF, in subsequent scene, is heard crying out)

(Cut to:)

MACDUFF.
>   Ahh!
>   My children too?

MALCOLM.
    Wife, children, servants, all
    That could be found.

MACDUFF.
    My wife killed too?

MALCOLM.
    I have said.
    Be comforted.
    Let's make us medicines of our great revenge
    To cure this deadly grief.

MACDUFF.
    He has no children.
    All my pretty ones? Did you say all?
    O hell-kite! All? What, all my pretty chickens
    And their dam, at one fell swoop?

MALCOLM.
    Dispute it like a man.

MACDUFF.
    I shall do so;
    But I must also feel it as a man.
    I cannot but remember such things were
    That were most precious to me. Did Heaven look
    And would not take their part? Sinful Macduff
    They were all struck for thee.
    Naught for their own demerits but for thine
    Fell slaughter on their souls.
    Heaven rest them now.

MALCOLM.
    Be this the whetstone of your sword
    Let grief convert to anger. Blunt not the heart.
    Enrage it.

MACDUFF.
    O, I could play the woman with mine eyes
    And braggart with my tongue! But, gentle heavens

Cut short all intermission. Front to front
Bring thou this fiend of Scotland and myself.
Within my sword's length set him; if he scape,
Heaven forgive him too.

(Blackout. LADY MACBETH discovers WITCHES
removing LADY MACDUFF gear)

LADY MACBETH. (angrily)
Beldams,
Saucy and over-bold? How did you dare
To trade and traffick with Macbeth
In riddles and affairs of death,
And I, the mistress of your charms,
The close contriver of all harms,
Was never called to bear my part,
Or show the glory of our art?
Thou shalt make amends: now get you gone.

(Exits)

1ST WITCH.
Come, let's make haste; she'll soon be back again.

(1ST WITCH, using twig, draws a circle on the ground.
2ND and 3RD WITCHES place effigy of LADY MAC-
BETH in centre. WITCHES then chant the following,
reinforced with tape in background:
'Double, double, toil, trouble
Fire burn, cauldron bubble'
This is endlessly repeated as WITCHES, facing effigy,
twitch thumbs in a repeated rhythm and slowly kneel
before it. On a signal, they abruptly end their chant.
Each WITCH, taking her turn, jabs a sharp, silver
knitting-needle into the effigy's head. Pause. The
perforated effigy sways gently for a moment in its
frame. Then the 1ST WITCH tears off a piece of the
effigy's heart revealing blood-red colouring underneath.
2ND WITCH tears off another strip from the effigy's
leg. Blood-red colouring revealed again. 3RD
WITCH tears off a strip from effigy's head. Blood-
red colouring revealed again. Pause. WITCHES
stand silently watching the torn effigy swaying in its

frame. Suddenly, the effigy is removed by WITCHES 2 & 3. 1ST WITCH cocks her head hearing someone's approach and backs slowly up-stage as she says)

1ST WITCH.
By the pricking of my thumbs,
Something wicked this way comes.

(2ND WITCH, now playing GENTLEWOMAN, enters with DOCTOR)

DOCTOR. When was it she last walked?

GENTLEWOMAN. Since his majesty went into the field I have seen her rise from her bed, throw her nightgown upon her, unlock her closet, take forth paper, fold it, write upon't, read it, afterwards seal it, and again return to bed; yet all this while in a most fast sleep.

DOCTOR. In this slumbery agitation, besides her walking and other actual performances, what, at any time, have you heard her say?

GENTLEWOMAN. That, sir, which I will not report after her.

DOCTOR. You may to me; and 'tis most meet you should.

GENTLEWOMAN. Neither to you nor anyone, having no witness to confirm my speech.

(Enter LADY MACBETH with a taper)

Look you! Here she comes. This is her very guise; and, upon my life, fast asleep. Observe her; stand close.

DOCTOR. How came she by that light?

GENTLEWOMAN. Why, it stood by her. She has light by her continually; 'tis her command.

DOCTOR. You see her eyes are open.

GENTLEWOMAN. Ay, but their sense are shut.

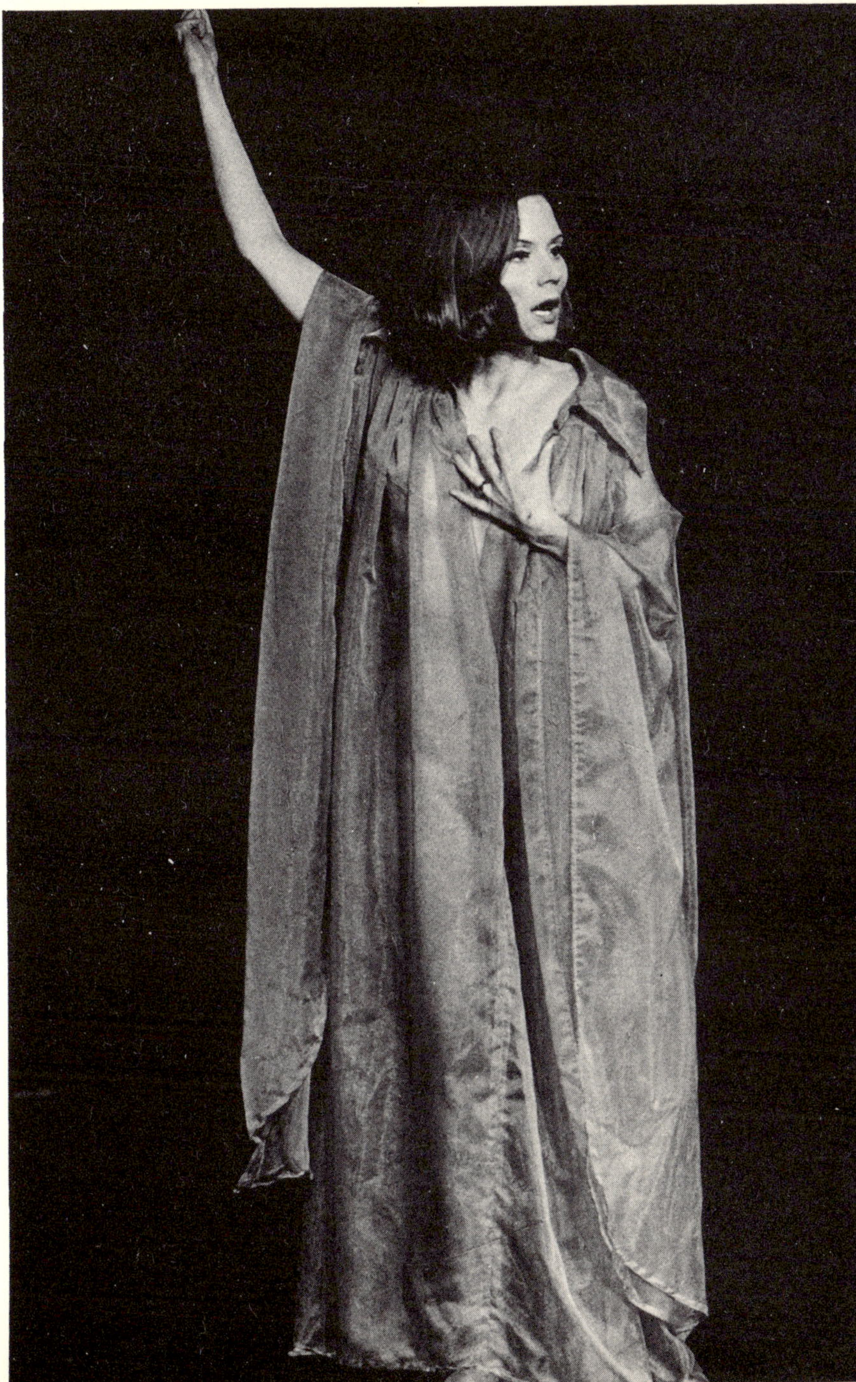

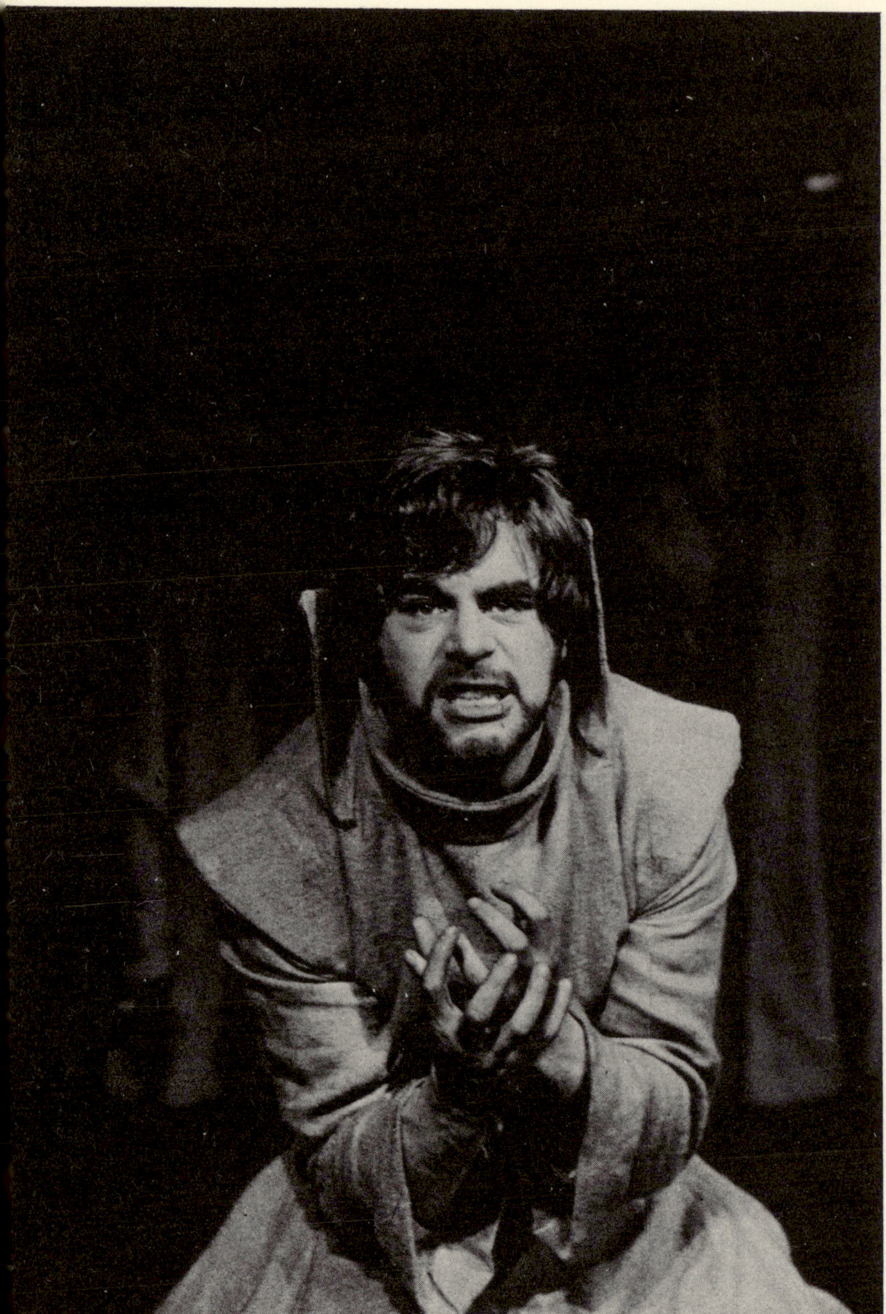

DOCTOR.
   What is it she does now? Look how she rubs her hands.

GENTLEWOMAN.
   It is an accustomed action with her to seem thus
   washing her hands. I have known her continue in
   this a quarter of an hour.

LADY MACBETH.
   Yet here's a spot.

   (DOCTOR ushers GENTLEWOMAN off. WITCHES,
   at side, deal with LADY MACBETH effigy throughout
   scene. LADY MACBETH wears transparent night-
   dress. Carries a long taper)

LADY MACBETH	WITCHES.
Out, damned spot! Out I say.	Fillet of a fenny snake In the cauldron boil and bake
One: two: why then, 'tis time to do't. Hell is murky - Fie, my lord, fie. A Soldier and a'feared? - What need we fear who knows it, when none can call our power to account? - Yet who would have thought the old man to have so much blood in him?	
The Thane of Fife had a wife; where is she now? - What, will these hands ne'er be clean.	Eye of newt and toe of frog, Wool of bat, and tongue of dog, Adder's fork and blind- worm's sting Lizard's leg and howleg's wing,
No more o' that my	

Lord, no more o'
that. You mar all
with this
starting. Here's the
smell of
blood still. All the
perfumes
of Arabia will not
sweeten this
little hand. Oh! Oh!.
Oh!

Ohhhhhhhhhhhhhhhhhhhh
(Sympathetic cry turns
shrill and cruel)

Wash your hands; put on
your night-
gown; look not so pale.
I tell
you again, Banquo's
buried; he
cannot come out on's
grave.

(taking her round)
To bed, to bed.

(Resisting slightly)
There's a
knocking at the gate.

Come, come, come, come,
give
me your hand.

What's done cannot be
undone.

To bed, to bed, to bed.

(They shroud her over in
their costumes, snuff out
her light, and carry her
away)

(A funeral procession. A coffin carrying the corpse
of LADY MACBETH enters and is set downstage.
Surrounding the bier are the WITCHES, MACBETH and
a PRIEST. After a moment's mumbled prayer, the
PRIEST comes forward and delivers the eulogy)

PRIEST.
>Tomorrow and tomorrow and tomorrow
>Creeps in this petty pace from day to day
>To the last syllable of recorded time
>And all our yesterdays have lighted fools
>The way to dusty death. Out, out, brief candle
>Life's but a walking shadow; a poor player
>That struts and frets his hour upon the stage
>And then is heard no more. It is a tale
>Told by an idiot, full of sound and fury
>Signifying nothing.

>(The PRIEST crosses himself. There is a moment's silence. MACBETH looks dazed. He crouches down beside the bier to peer intently into the corpse's eyes. Then, suddenly angered, he turns and goes. The others also move off leaving the three WITCHES hovering over the coffin. After a moment, the 1ST WITCH bends down to take up LADY MACBETH's crown. The others struggle with her for a moment. She pushes them away. Then very slowly she places the crown onto her head and gazes imperiously out towards the audience. The other two WITCHES keep their eyes riveted on her. The lights slowly fade out)

>(Cut to: MALCOLM and MACDUFF on two platforms above. In centre, MACBETH is seated on throne. He looks straight out, fear in his eyes. Clustered around the throne is a fresco of heads - all the characters of the play. They intone a dull, smouldering sound - barely audible - while MALCOLM's and MACDUFF's speeches are played out)

MACDUFF.
>O Scotland, Scotland!
>O nation miserable,
>With an untitled tyrant, bloody-sceptred,
>When shalt thou see thy wholesome days again?

MALCOLM.
>Our country sinks beneath the yoke.
>It weeps, it bleeds, and each new day a gash

Is added to her wounds.
Each new morn
New widows howl, new orphans cry, new sorrows
Strike heaven on the face, that it resounds
As if it felt with Scotland, and yelled out
Like syllable of dolour.

MACDUFF.
Alas poor country!
Almost afraid to know itself! It cannot
Be called our mother, but our grave; where nothing
But who-knows-nothing is once seen to smile;
Where sighs and groans and shrieks that rent the air
Are made not marked; where violent sorrow seems
A modern ecstasy.

What I believe I'll wail;
What know, believe; and what I can redress,
As I shall find the time to friend, I will.

MALCOLM.
This tyrant whose sole name blisters our tongue!
Not in the legions
Of horrid hell can come a devil more damned
In evils to top Macbeth.
Some say he's mad.

MACDUFF.
Others that lesser hate him
Do call it valiant fury; but for certain
He cannot buckle his distempered cause
Within the belt of rule.

MALCOLM.
Now does he feel
His secret murders sticking on his hands;

MACDUFF.
Now, minutely, revolts upbraid his faith-breach.

MALCOLM.
Those he commands move only in command,
Nothing in love.

MACDUFF.
> Now does he feel his title
> Hang loose about him like a giant's robe
> Upon a dwarfish thief.

MALCOLM.
> Who then shall blame
> His pestered senses to recoil and start,
> When all that is within him does condemn
> Itself for being there?

MACDUFF.
> Well, march we now
> To give obedience where till truly owed.

MALCOLM.
> Gracious England hath
> Lent us good Seyward and ten thousand men -

MACDUFF.
> Our power is ready;
> Our lack is nothing but our leave.

MALCOLM.
> Macbeth
> Is ripe for shaking, and the powers above
> Put on their instruments.

MACDUFF.
> Forward
> Make we our march towards Birnam!

(During the scene, the drone has steadily increased in volume. On MACDUFF's last speech it bursts into a wild, chaotic clamour. Blackout)

(On lights up: All are circled around the perimeter of the stage facing outward - like pillars of a human fortress. They all hold witches' brooms as if they were spears. MACBETH, with sword, in centre. During the next dialogue, each actor turns downstage centre to deliver his line. It is shouted out as if it were a message being called out from a great distance)

2ND MACBETH.
    The night has been unruly.

BANQUO.
    Chimneys were blown down.

MALCOLM.
    Lamentings heard i' the air.

3RD MACBETH.
    Strange screams of death
    And prophesying with accents terrible
    Of fire combustion and confused events.

MACBETH.
    The mind I sway by and the heart I bear
    Shall never sag with doubt nor shake with fear.

MALCOLM.
    Foul whisperings are abroad.

MACDUFF.
    The English power is near.
    Led on by Malcolm.

MACBETH.
    What's the boy Malcolm?
    Was he not born of woman?

(All beat the floor with broom-handles; three knocks)

Who's there?

2ND MACBETH.
    A farmer that hanged himself
    on the expectation of plenty.

MACBETH. (to himself)
    Why should I play the Roman fool and die
    On mine own sword? Whiles I see lives, the gashes
    Do better upon them.

(shouting orders)
Send out more horses; skirr the country round
Hang those that talk of fear.
Who's there?

(Three knocks)

DUNCAN.
Old Seyward and ten thousand men.

MACBETH.
Hang out our banners on the outward walls.
Our castle's strength
Will laugh a siege to scorn.

LADY MACBETH. (off-stage)
What is that noise?

DUNCAN.
It was owl that shriek'd, the fatal bellman
Which gives the stern'st good-night.

(Three knocks)

MACBETH.
Who's there?

DUNCAN.
Old Seyward and ten thousand men.

2ND MACBETH. (kneeling as MESSENGER)
All is confirmed, my lord, which was reported.

(MACBETH, shaken, rises from throne and takes a few steps forward; is caught up in LADY MACBETH's arms)

MACBETH.
Dearest chuck.

LADY MACBETH. (as mother)
Put this night's great business into my dispatch.

MACBETH. (holding her desperately)
    I have lived long enough; my way of life
    Is fallen into the sere, the yellow leaf;
    And that which should accompany old age,
    As honour, love, obedience, troops of friends,
    I must not look to have.

LADY MACBETH.
    Poor prattler, how thou talk'st.

MACBETH.
    There's nothing serious in mortality.
    All is but toys. Renown and grace is dead.
    The wine of life is drawn and the mere lees
    Is left this vault to brag of.
    Naught's had, all's spent...

LADY MACBETH.
    Consider it not so deeply.

MACBETH.
    I am in blood.
    Stepped in so far, that should I wade no more
    Returning were as tedious as go o'er.

LADY MACBETH. (cuddling him)
    You lack the season of all natures, sleep.

MACBETH. (held tight in LADY MACBETH's arms)
    It will have blood, they say; blood will have blood.
    Stones have been known to move and trees to speak;
    Augurs and understood relations have,
    By maggot-pies, and choughs and rooks brought forth
    The secret'st man of blood.

LADY MACBETH. (consoling)
    What's done is done.

MACBETH. (suddenly turning)
    Canst thou not minister to a mind diseased,
    And with some sweet, oblivious antidote
    Cleanse the stuffed bosom of that perilous stuff
    Which weighs upon the heart.

LADY MACBETH.
> These deeds must not be thought
> After these ways, so it will make us mad.
> Blood hath been shed ere now, i' the olden time,
> Ere human statute purged the gentle weal;
> Ay, and since too, murders have been performed
> Too terrible for the ear. We are yet but young in deed.
>
> But fear not,
> Yet shalt thou take upon you what is yours.

MACBETH. (bucked)
> Bring forth men-children only,
> For thy undaunted mettle should compose
> Nothing but males.
> We will establish our estate upon
> Our eldest; and signs of nobleness,
> Like stars, shall shine
> On all deservers.
> (turns to her)
> My dearest partner of greatness.

(MACBETH goes to kiss LADY MACBETH. Curiously, she resists; he looks at her quizzically wondering why her tenderness has vanished. LADY MACBETH looks him squarely in the eyes. Transforms)

LADY MACBETH.
> The queen, my lord, is dead.

(She becomes immobile. The WITCHES suddenly appear and remove her body. A shriek is heard off-stage)

2ND MACBETH.
> Gracious my lord,
> I should report that which I say I saw,
> But know not how to do't.

MACBETH. (hysterical)
> Well, say, sir!

2ND MACBETH.
    As I did stand my watch upon the hill
    I looked toward Birnam and anon me thought
    The wood began to move.

MACBETH.
    Liar and slave. If thou speakest false
    Upon the next tree shalt thou hang. If thy speech be sooth
    I care not if thou durst for me as much.
    Arm, arm and out I gin to be aweary of the sun
    And wish the estate of the world were now undone.
    Ring the alarum bell.
    They have tied me to a stake. I cannot fly
    But bear-like I must fight the course.
    Ring the alarum bell.

(The circle which had been facing up-stage, slowly turns downstage to face MACBETH. Each character holds a witch's broom. There is a long, electric pause as circle confronts MACBETH. Then they begin to tighten around him. MACBETH draws one of his daggers. As each character comes forward, he strikes at his broomstick; the character drops broom and retires)

    What's he
    That was not born of woman? Such a one
    Am I to fear or none.

(MACDUFF suddenly turns to confront MACBETH. He, unlike all the others in the circle, holds a sword)

MACDUFF.
    If thou be'st slain and with no stroke of mine,
    My wife and children's ghosts will haunt me still.

MACBETH.
    Of all men else I have avoided thee.
    But get thee back; my soul is too much charged
    With blood of thine already.

MACDUFF.
>I have no words;
>My voice is in my sword, thou bloodier villain
>Than terms can give thee out.

(They duel. MACDUFF weakens)

MACBETH.
>Thou losest labour.
>Let fall thy blade on vulnerable crests,
>I bear a charmed life which must not yield
>To one of woman born.

MACDUFF.
>Despair thy charm
>And let the angel whom thou still hast served
>Tell thee Macduff was from his mother's womb
>Untimely ripped.

MACBETH.
>Accursed be that tongue that tells me so
>For it hath cow'd my better part of man:
>And be these juggling fiends no more believed
>That palter with us in a double sense
>That keep the word of promise to our ear
>And break it to our hope. I'll not fight with thee.

MACDUFF.
>Then yield thee coward,
>And live to be the show and gaze of the time.
>We'll have thee, as our rarer monsters are,
>Painted upon a pole, and underwrit:
>"Here may you see the tyrant!"

(All characters now rise up with their brooms and stalk MACBETH. MACBETH stands frozen and helpless. When he is completely surrounded, all begin to beat him to death with broomsticks. This done, MACDUFF approaches the heap. As he does so, MACBETH's effigy becomes visible again; beside it, back to the audience, stands LADY MACBETH. As

MACDUFF raises his sword over the heap, LADY
MACBETH raises her instrument over the effigy's
head. As MACDUFF strikes, LADY MACBETH
dashes off the head of the effigy. The tight circle
surrounding MACBETH widens and opens. MACBETH
is laying in a heap, a black-sack over his head.
All exit but three WITCHES. WITCHES silently commune
with each other then slowly come downstage and take off
their stocking-masks)

1ST WITCH. (simply, conversationally)
When shall we three meet again?
In thunder, lightning or in rain?

2ND WITCH.
When the hurly-burly's done,
When the battle's lost and won.

3RD WITCH.
That will be 'ere the set of sun.

(WITCHES stand motionless. The battery of lights
that line the back of the stage slowly come to full
then fade to black)

C AND B PLAYSCRIPTS

		Cloth	Paper
*PS 1	TOM PAINE by Paul Foster	21s	9s0d
*PS 2	BALLS and other plays (The Recluse, Hurrah for the Bridge The Hessian Corporal) by Paul Foster	25s	10s0d
PS 3	THREE PLAYS (Lunchtime Concert, Coda The Inhabitants) by Olwen Wymark	21s	7s0d
*PS 4	CLEARWAY by Vivienne C. Welburn	21s	7s0d
*PS 5	JOHNNY SO LONG and THE DRAG by Vivienne C. Welburn	25s	9s0d
*PS 6	SAINT HONEY and OH DAVID, ARE YOU THERE? by Paul Ritchie	25s	11s0d
PS 7	WHY BOURNEMOUTH? and other plays (The Missing Links, An Apple a Day) by John Antrobus	25s	10s0d
*PS 8	THE CARD INDEX and other plays (The Interrupted Act, Gone Out) by Tadeusz Rozewicz trans. Adam Czerniawski	25s	11s0d
PS 9	US by Peter Brook and others	42s	21s0d

			Cloth	Paper
*PS 10	SILENCE and THE LIE by Nathalie Sarraute trans. Maria Jolas		25s	9s0d
*PS 11	THE WITNESSES and other plays (The Old Woman Broods, The Funny Old Man) by Tadeusz Rozewicz trans. Adam Czerniawski		30s	12s0d
*PS 12	THE CENCI by Antonin Artaud trans. Simon Watson-Taylor		18s	8s0d
*PS 13	PRINCESS IVONA by Witold Combrowicz trans. Krystyna Griffith-Jones and Catherine Robins		21s	9s0d
*PS 14	WIND IN THE BRANCHES OF THE SASSAFRAS by Rene de Obaldia trans. Joseph Foster		25s	9s0d
*PS 15	INSIDE OUT and other plays (Talking of Michaelangelo, Still Fires, Rofley's Grave, Come Tomorrow) by Jan Quackenbush		21s	9s0d
*PS 16	THE SWALLOWS by Roland Dubillard trans. Barbara Wright		25s	9s0d
PS 17	THE DUST OF SUNS by Raymond Roussel trans. Lane Dunlop		25s	9s0d
PS 18	EARLY MORNING by Edward Bond		25s	9s0d

		Cloth	Paper
PS 19	THE HYPOCRITE by Robert McLellan	25s	10s0d
PS 20	THE BALACHITES and THE STRANGE CASE OF MARTIN RICHTER by Stanley Eveling	30s	12s0d
PS 21	A SEASON IN THE CONGO by Aime Cesaire	25s	9s0d
PS 22	TRIXIE AND BABA by John Antrobus	21s	9s0d
PS 23	SPRING AWAKENING by Frank Wedekind trans. Tom Osborn	25s	9s0d
*PS 24	PRECIOUS MOMENTS FROM THE FAMILY ALBUM TO PROVIDE YOU WITH COMFORT IN THE LONG YEARS TO COME by Naftali Yavin	25s	9s0d
*PS 25	DESIRE CAUGHT BY THE TAIL by Pablo Picasso trans. Roland Penrose	18s	8s0d
*PS 26	THE BREASTS OF TIRESIAS by Guillaume Apollinaire	18s	8s0d
PS 27	ANNA LUSE and other plays (Jens, Purity) by David Mowat	30s	15s0d
*PS 28	O and other plays by Sandro Key-Aberg	30s	15s0d
*PS 29	WELCOME TO DALLAS, MR. KENNEDY Kaj Himmelstrup	25s	9s0d

			Cloth	Paper
PS 30	THE LUNATIC, THE SECRET SPORTSMAN AND THE WOMEN NEXT DOOR and VIBRATIONS by Stanley Eveling		30s	12s0d
*PS 31	STRINDBERG by Colin Wilson		21s	9s0d
*PS 32	THE FOUR LITTLE GIRLS by Pablo Picasso trans. Roland Penrose		25s	10s0d
PS 33	MACRUNE's GUEVARA by John Spurling		25s	9s0d
*PS 34	THE MARRIAGE by Witold Gombrowicz trans. Louis Iribarne		35s	15s0d
*PS 35	BLACK OPERA and THE GIRL WHO BARKS LIKE A DOG by Gabriel Cousin trans. Irving Lycett		30s	15s0d
*PS 36	SAWNEY BEAN by Robert Nye and Bill Watson		25s	10s0d
PS 37	COME AND BE KILLED and DEAR JANET ROSENBERG, DEAR MRS KOONING by Stanley Eveling		35s	15s0d
PS 38	VIETNAM DISCOURSE by Peter Weiss trans. Geoffrey Skelton		42s	21s0d

		Cloth	Paper
*PS 39	HEIMSKRINGLA or THE STONED ANGELS by Paul Foster	30s	12s0d
*PS 40	JAN PALACH by Alan Burns	25s	9s0d
*PS 41	HOUSE OF BONES by Roland Dubillard	35s	15s0d
*PS 42	THE TREADWHEEL and COIL WITHOUT DREAMS by Vivienne C. Welburn	25s	9s0d
PS 43	THE NUNS by Eduardo Manet trans. Robert Baldick	25s	10s0d
PS 44	THE SLEEPERS DEN and OVER GARDENS OUT by Peter Gill	25s	10s0d
PS 45	A MACBETH by Charles Marowitz	30s	12s0d
PS 46	SLEUTH by Anthony Shaffer	25s	10s0d
*PS 47	SAMSON and ALISON MARY FAGAN by David Selbourne	25s	10s0d
*PS 48	OPERETTA by Witold Gombrowicz trans. Louis Iribarne	25s	10s0d
*PS 49	THE NUTTERS and other plays (Social Service, A Cure for Souls) by A. F. Cotterell	25s	10s0d

		Cloth	Paper
PS 50	THE GYMNASIUM and other plays (The Technicians, Stay Where You Are, Jack the Giant-Killer) by Olwen Wymark	25s	10s0d
PS 51	THREE PLAYS (The Sword, The Man in the Green Muffler, In Transit) by Stewart Conn	25s	10s0d
*PS 52	COINS and other plays (The Good Shine, Calcium, Broken) by Jan Quackenbush	25s	10s0d
*PS 53	FOUR BLACK REVOLUTIONARY PLAYS (Experimental Death Unit 1, A Black Mass, Madheart, Great Goodness of Life) by Leroi Jones	25s	10s0d
PS 54	LONG VOYAGE OUT OF WAR by Ian Curteis	42s	21s0d
PS 55	INUIT and THE OTHERS by David Mowat	25s	10s0d
PS 56	COUNCIL OF LOVE by Oscar Panizza trans. and adapted by John Bird	30s	12s0d

*All plays marked thus are represented for dramatic presentation by:
C and B (Theatre) Ltd, 18 Brewer Street, London W1